Contents

Editorial

П1 **What's the Point?**
Nina Bilbey

П2 **Revert to type**
Michael Paraskos

П3 **Further thoughts on carving**
Matthew Rowe

П4 **Percussion versus Rotation: Masonry, Stonecarving and Technology**
Tim Crawley

П5 **Dissociation:**
Michael Paraskos

П6 **Coming of Age in Carving**
Takako Jin

П7 **Carving in Wood and Stone**
Tony Webb

П8 **Interview with Jon Isherwood**
Michael Paraskos

ПΥΓΜΑΛΙΩΝ

provocations in contemporary carving

2

EDITORIAL   Can you carve a mushroom cloud?

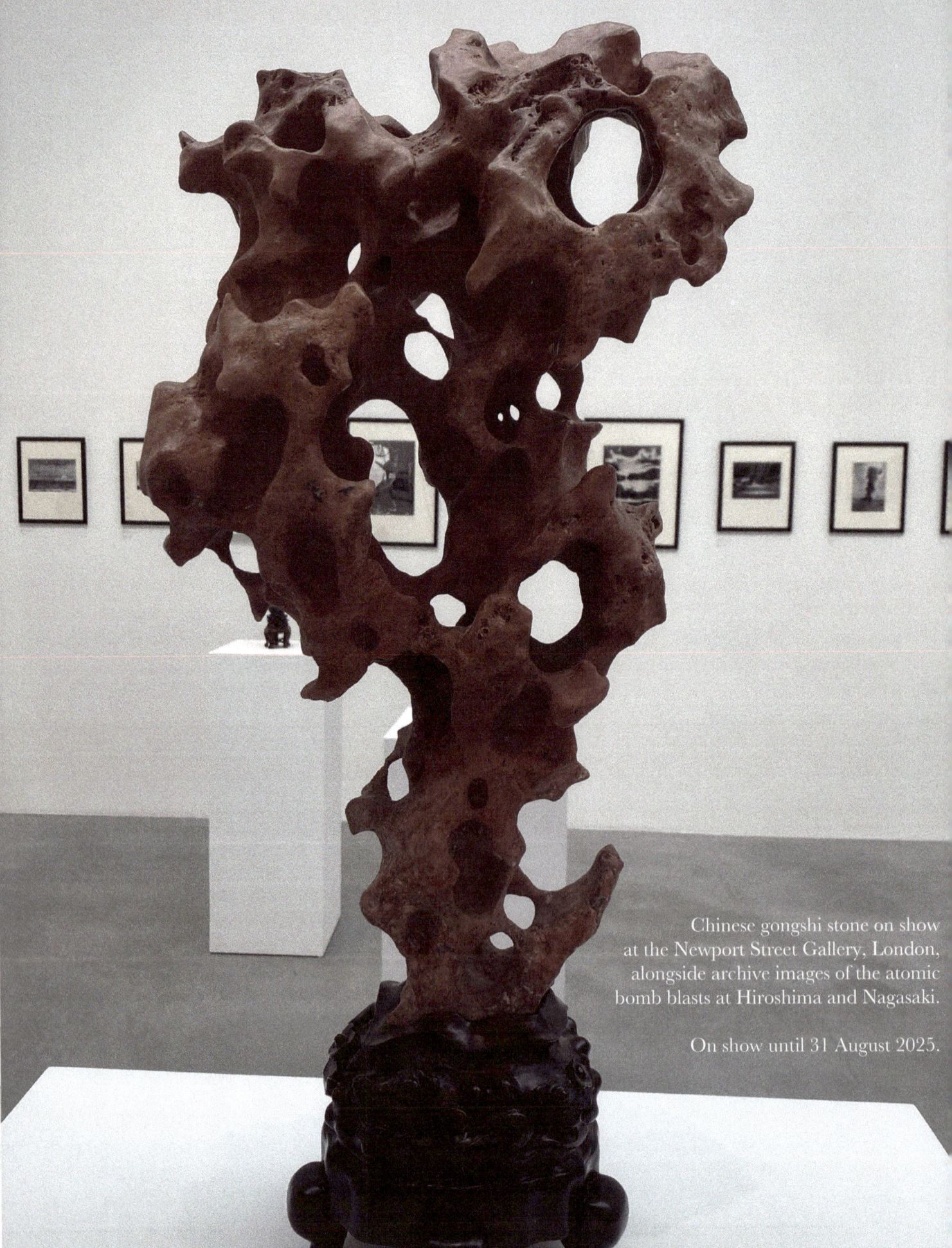

Chinese gongshi stone on show at the Newport Street Gallery, London, alongside archive images of the atomic bomb blasts at Hiroshima and Nagasaki.

On show until 31 August 2025.

We have been joking about this being the difficult second album. I have been publishing this-and-that on-and-off since childhood, from the time when my brother, Christopher, and I would hand draw copies of a comic we called *The Cat's Mouth*. I would have been about seven years old. Even that was a kind of art magazine insofar as it featured artists and art students, all summer visitors to the Cyprus College of Art, founded by my father. But we didn't talk about art. We made childishly rude comic strips, usually about everyone getting drunk all the time.

As a Dada-ist joke I still like the idea of an art magazine that doesn't mention art. As a lot of art history is written like that anyway, why not have a contemporary art magazine that just talks about the drunken antics of artists or who's sleeping with whom? As a passing fancy it would be childishly amusing, a piece of diverting escapism in a troubled world, like art's version of *Closer* magazine.

My first real journal was very much about art. Or, rather, it was about poetry. As a student at the University of Leeds I accidentally became editor of what was already a venerable poetry magazine, *Poetry and Audience*. But my editorial debut was not so much a cat's mouth as a pig's ear. I was left on my own to create something with neither the necessary experience nor real understanding to succeed. There was not much sympathy for my naivity from the University authorities when I failed spectacularly, and I was soon asked to leave as editor while being very publicly blamed for my incompetence.

Apart from a sharp lesson in institutional cruelty, what I did learn from *Poetry and Audience* was that even if a small-circulation magazine has a long history, its individual editors might not last long. For most small magazines, however, the sad truth is that the journal itself will fold soon after launch. As anyone who has ever browsed the depository of modernist art and poetry magazines that have been scanned and placed online by the wonderful Modernist Journals Project, this brevity is a common feature of this kind of journal. Consequently it will be no surprise to learn that my third magazine, another art and poetry publication, called *The Tempest*, lasted three issues. So did my fourth, called *ArtCyprus*. And so, as I look at the tangerine-coloured cover of this issue of *Pygmalion*, I find myself wondering if there will ever be an issue three, let alone four.

I suppose there are three things that will determine that. The first is that I and others continue in our willingness to put time, energy and money into producing it. These are precious resources, although I have no reason at the moment to think they will run out, as long as people are also willing to write for us (that is a very heavy hint to you — *dear Reader* — why not write something for us?).

The second is that *Pygmalion* continues to be needed as a place where we do not just celebrate the act of carving in all its diverse forms, but we challenge, question and confront some of the assumptions about carving that seem to risk rendering it redundant as an activity in the modern world. What I mean by that unless we argue a cogent case for carving to continue it could easily turn into one of those zombie hobby crafts pursued only by amateurs, at which point the only journal of any value would be called *Leisure Carver*.

And third? That is much more simple — it is that human civilization does not collapse at the hands of climate emergency deniers, still pumping vast quantities carbon dioxide and methane into the air, and polluting land and sea. Or that we do not explode in a blinding light as some maniacal leader unleases yet another war on a hurting world. It is a controversial point, but I suspect in the event of nuclear annihilation we might at least suspend publication of the next issue of *Pygmalion*.

That might seem like a *non sequitur* — why suddenly bring in the the threat of nuclear war to a discussion as to why a journal like *Pygmalion* is needed? But to my mind it is the very opposite of a *non sequitur* (so I suppose it is a *sequitur*). Carving is not some innocent virgin, to be locked away like Danaë in a brass tower to avoid it being sullied by the dirty reality of the quotidian world. To be relevant it must be part of the world. In fact it cannot really avoid it. Like everything else it affects and is affected by reality, and so the presence of nuclear-armed megalomaniacs determined to make life miserable for so many people, and the levels of social injustice we now have across the world, and the mass extinction of life being caused by deforestation, global heating and the pollution of air, land and water is relevant to carving because it is relevant to everything. We just (just!) need to work out how it is relevant.

As an historian I would put this into context by asking that we remember how in Europe's golden age of carving, the Middle Ages, carvers engaged absolutely with the world around them. They did this by carving for God. This was never an act of escapism. The medieval world was a religious world in which an immanent God mattered and so carving mattered as it engaged with God. Translating that principle into our world, where religion is probably not a driving force for most people, perhaps the purpose of a publication like *Pygmalion* is to ask what is now the equivalent mode of worldly engagement for carvers? Put another way, what makes carving relevant now? An answer to that question might well be the salvation of carving, and certainly a topic for the difficult third album.

Π1 PROVOCATION 1

What's the point?
The role of the pointing machine in a risk averse world
by Nina Bilbey

The three questions most frequently asked a carver:

1. Is this real stone?
2. How long did it take?
3. What do you do if you break a bit off?

My answer to the third question depends on who's asking and has evolved over the years to "I try not to." Where does this universal obsession with carvers making a mistake come from? Perhaps the observer wants us to share an ancient secret, something only spoken of in circles of the initiated. For the record, I make mistakes frequently, one so serious it nearly killed me, but often there is no secret - it just needs a two-part epoxy glue, a sit down and a choice swear word.

Mistakes and accepting the possibility of failure is a familiar part of carving, but the value of taking risks is seldom recognised as an important part of learning. Sometimes you can work for days or weeks and feel like you're progressing well only to understand that you've pushed something too far.

But in doing so you've understood what 'too far' looks and, more importantly, feels like. I am talking about how incremental risk might lead to a mistake, but could also lead to faster proficiency and a better outcome. We all need to be pushed out of our comfort zone and asked to carve a little faster; to be shown, especially at the beginning of a carving career, how to hit a chisel slightly harder to achieve a more confident surface and to see a little deeper into the material. This shift to accept risk, particularly for those with little experience of failure, can mark a crucial step on a journey in this historic craft.

So where's the point?

In our pursuit to learn skills quickly with guaranteed results and low risk, the carver will often be on the lookout for tricks that can speed up the roughing out process. We build scale frames, invent measuring tools like proportional callipers, employ new technology like scanning and mechanical milling.

But one 'aid' stands out as the most mysterious, the pointing machine.

Unlike the pantograph, an instrument that can reduce and enlarge measurements with the aid of a system of geared pins, the pointing machine helps reproduce a model the same size and proportion.

The machine, like the development of diamond cutting tools, was pivotal to stone carving technology. It opened the possibility of exact carved replicas for profit. The eighteenth-century engraver Nicolas-Marie Gatteaux is credited with its invention but it was commercialised by the sculptor John Bacon and perfected by Antonio Canova. The frame has fixed points that can be transferred from the original object to the material being carved, but it also has an adjustable and lockable 'pointing arm' that moves in and out to indicate where the surface stops. It is the parent of the 3D scanner, the child of the three-point triangulation technique used in Roman sculpture and is still the tool used in traditional studios reproducing carving from either original models or cast copies. Visit any of Pietrasanta's older carving studios and you will find the walls packed with plaster models covered with tiny, raised spots, evidence of years of continued use in the copying process. Although it fell out of fashion in the age of Hepworth and Moore, it has once more embedded itself in studio practice and in the hearts and minds of contemporary carvers including my own.

So, what does the pointing machine contribute to our workshops and more importantly what can it offer learners in the continued dance with risk versus failure?

The value to copying an object can be measured in several ways. Monetary and historical, but also what it teaches you. How it improves your understanding of carving. If you choose to copy a classical cast, and use the pointing machine to help, you put yourself in the mind of the original carver. You start to see through their eyes, to feel their skill channel through your own hands. It is seductive and exhilarating. The pointing machine gives you direct access to the design decisions made by others. The machine allows you to experience mastery and recognition. It allows you to show off. Making something beautiful and valuable can give a carver an injection of enthusiasm and validation desperately needed when practical gains are slow to materialise. All without risk.

Of course, the pointing machine cannot hide inexperience. To the skilled craftsperson when a learner picks up a tool and stands at the banker, we see you. I can be in another room and hear a person hit stone and know that person needs help. It is no wonder the pointing machine is so seductive. Like doping in sports, it allows you to perform at a level that is aspirational. Artificial. Yet it can put you in the room with other carvers in the commissioning arena. It can give you a start at a career. And that alone is a valid reason for its use.

My own relationship with the pointing machine is complicated. As someone largely self- taught, it presented itself as a tutor, standing over me. Encouraging me to jump ahead. It allowed me to hit stone harder, carve faster, way beyond my experience and natural ability. I have used the machine in nearly every commercial commission.

Brenda Putman in her fascinating book *The Sculptors Way: A Guide to Modelling and Sculpture* (Dover 1948) talks animatedly about the necessity of 'carvers being able to measure the surface of a plaster model accurately and be able to interpret information in equal measure like a musician interprets a score.

Using a pointing machine can hone these skills

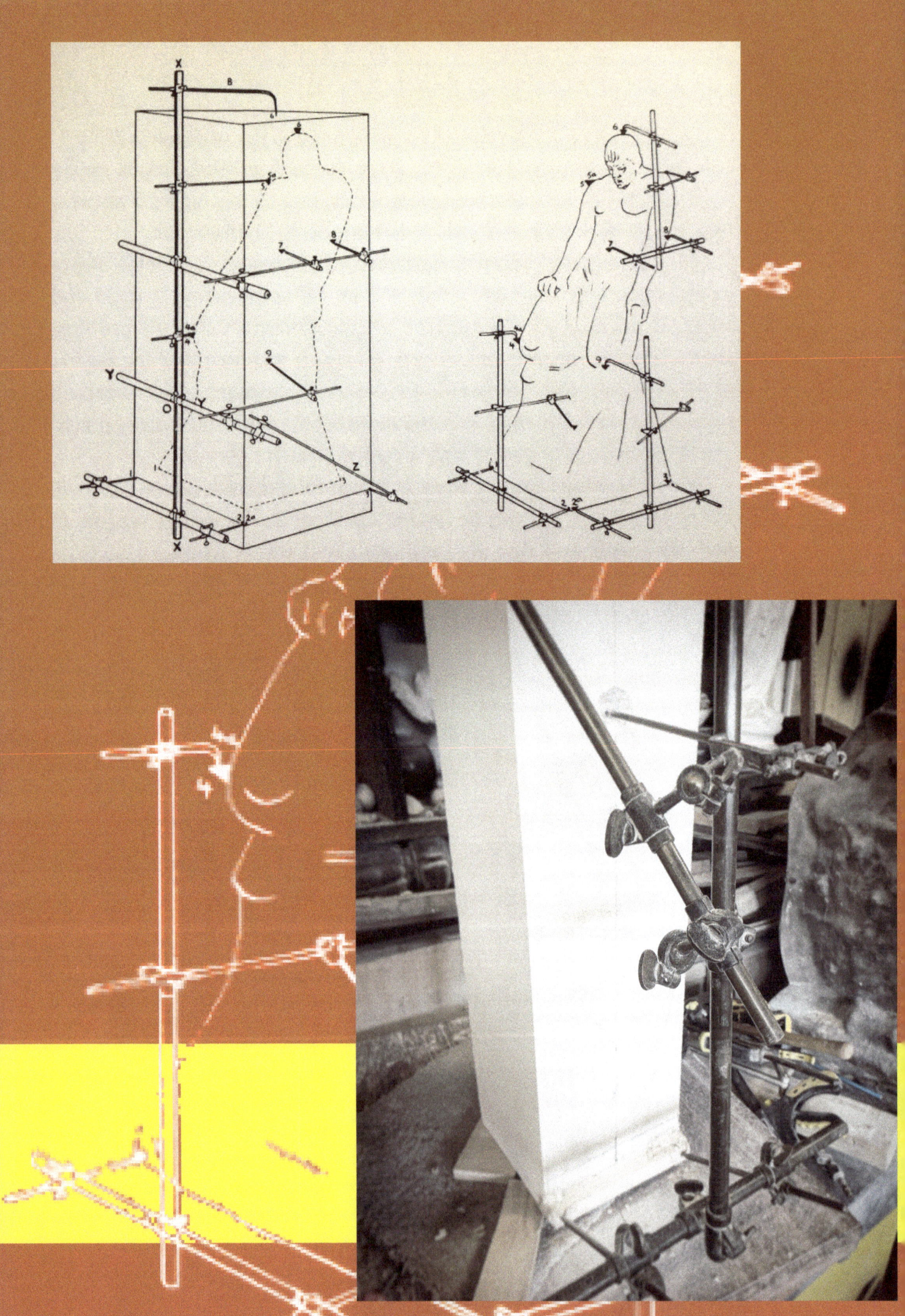

Like many people who start carving stone, initially I had no knowledge of the art of maquette making and the concept of copying a model. Direct carving was my 'thing' (carving without a one-to-one model). I started when I was 15, on blocks of cast plaster, drawing on the surface and responding as the shape developed. Direct carving is for me what cold-water swimming is to others. A scary thing that wakes you up. I truly inhabit my body when I'm direct carving, a part of my brain gets an electric jolt, a feeling that I don't experience anywhere else. And certainly, not when using the pointing machine.

Waking up

I've always been a fast carver, but the pointing machine made me slow up. At first, I thought that was good thing: constant checking and doubting what I saw would surely make me see more clearly and carve better. Over time I began to trust only the machine. Double checking every carving strike. I believed the model was the centre of the process, not the jumping off point. I devalued the carved object and elevated the model. Carving became repetitive and boring. On the surface I was making gorgeous classical copies but there was only one correct voice. And that wasn't mine. Eventually, my instincts were silenced, and I stopped direct carving altogether.

In an interview recently on *The Stone Carvers' and Letterers' Takeaway* podcast, Richard Kindersley spoke passionately of fear as a powerful motivator. An important emotion in making anything. Fear of failure in small aspects of your life allows you to problem solve and push boundaries. It makes you reflect and grow. Surrendering to your limitations as a carver can be terrifying but also transformative.

The sale of pointing machines is increasing as learners believe the machine will speed up their carving projects and reduce anxiety and pressure.

These are perfectly valid reasons for buying one, but the display of skill it offers is a mirage. (This is a safe place to be provocative, right?)

My hope is that anyone responding intuitively to a stone surface, producing exciting and slightly unresolved original works through a direct method, will think carefully before picking up a mechanical aid or a pointing machine. I am not arguing that the pointing machine has no place in the learning process or for the confident carver to stop using it to help with the reproduction of original works for commission. I am asking us to question how we should support learners and learn ourselves. Is it under the safe cloak of reproducing historic objects dependent on the pointing machine, or a tougher route involving greater risk and less resolution?

It wasn't until I read the first *Pygmalion,* I started to question why I chose to carve. Through re-examining my reasons and the effect carving had on my physical and mental state, I began to question how the use of the pointing machine and a mechanical act of reproduction played into that narrative. I began to realise the detrimental effect 'safe' tricks had on my enjoyment of carving and the overwhelming joy of taking risks and its unexpected outcomes. I try not to experience too much risk in other parts of my life, but direct carving feels like oxygen.

Maybe you are more confident with your boundaries around the machine than I was. And maybe direct carving isn't your thing. There's room for all, but there are choices, and those choices matter not only to your development and confidence as a carver, but to the larger questions around carving today.

In the the 1997 film *GI Jane,* Demi Moore famously adopted the term 'Failure is not an option'. I would suggest the carver's slogan should read 'failure to take risks is not an option'. I believe it to be the single most important element our lifelong journey to be happy and fulfilled carvers.

Nina Bilbey and Charlotte Howarth present regular podcast interviews with people from the world of carving.

Search for The Stonecarving Takeaway on Google or your usual podcast provider.

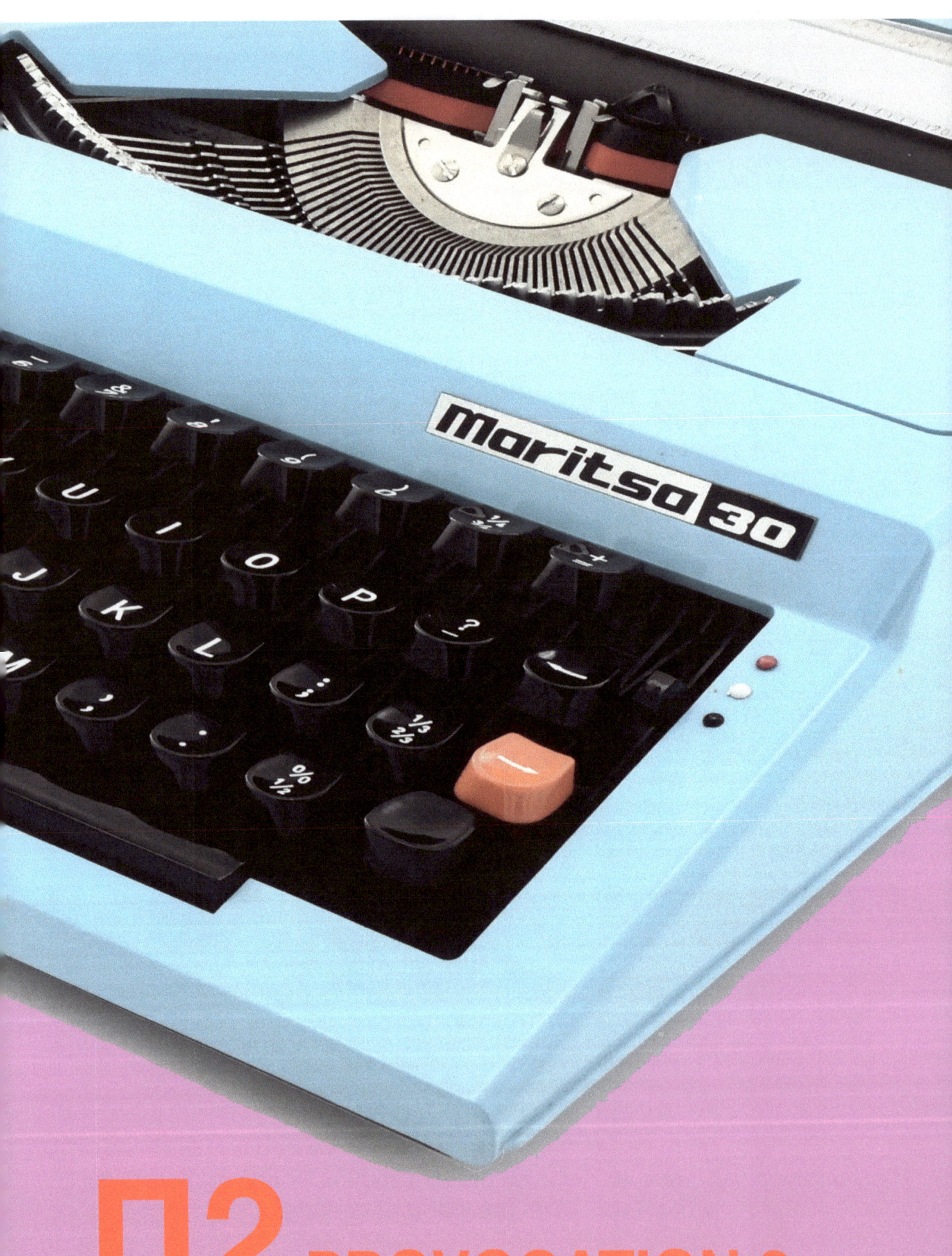

П2 PROVOCATION 2

Revert to type
by Michael Paraskos

This is an unusual article for me to write, not because of the subject matter, but due to my mode of writing - a manual **typewriter** - despite having been a user of word processors for thirty years or more, from their early appearance in my world in the guise of my brother's Commodore 64. That was borrowed to enable me to type my university dissertation myself, rather than following the more usual method of the time, of writing it by hand and paying someone to type it up. This money-saving wheeze resulted in a manuscript so full of errors I was told to rewrite it or risk failing my finals. Nonetheless it was a vision of the future, a glimpse of the coming age when everyone except the highest boss would have to type their own letters and memos (viz. emails) on a screen, and job titles like 'typist' and 'secretary' would seem as anachronistic as 'cooper' and 'doffer'. If only I knew it then, a world was opening up before me in which we would all be secretaries, or do I mean doffers?

But I digress. As I mentioned, this is an unusual article for me to write as it is written and composed on a manual **typewriter**. With it I have abandoned the digital age, and while it is not quite a return to quill and ink, the process feels very much like a momentous rejection of modern technology. It is not even an electric typewriter, it is a rather pretty ziggurat blue Maritsa 30, made in Bulgaria some time in the 1970s, and excellently light and portable for use by any Bulgarian double agent of that time needing to send coded memos (viz. emails) to Darzhavna sigurnost (secret service) headquarters in Sofia. It is in fact such a pretty little machine I wonder if it might not in fact be a honeytrap typewriter designed to lure 007 into revealing his secrets on its keys.

As it is, this Maritsa 30 is lumbered with me, but to my absolute amazement I can still type. I am making a few mistakes, but far fewer than I anticipated, and I am still relatively fast. But the point about me returning to a typewriter is not to test whether I still have what it takes to make it in the typing pool at Sunshine Desserts. If I am honest when I first attempted to return to a typewriter, in an aborted effort to resurect a long-abandoned Brother 3600 Electric typewriter I found in a cupboard at Imperial College, where it must once have been the latest thing in technology, I was not sure why I wanted to return to this old school technology. My experiment with the Brother 3600 ended when I received a rather nasty electric shock as I attempted to write a letter to Richard Barnes. Of course, I do not blame Richard for exposing me to the dangers of obsolete electrical wiring, but had he not first sent me a typed letter produced on a manual typewriter he had, apparently, received as a Christmas gift as a child, I doubt it would even have occured to me to try typing for myself. Typing was not therefore a foregone conclusion. That being the case, why did I spend £35 on an ex-communist 1970s manual typewriter, safely unelectric, to continue with this experiment? The answer is both mundanely simple and strangely remarkable. To me at least, and in all I say or write I can only ever speak for me.

The mundane answer is that, typing my letter to Richard on that deadly Brother 3600 exposed me to an experience of writing which felt extraordinarily new. New now, I mean. It was an experience of writing that I must have had using a typewriter three decades ago, but that experience was long forgotten. The mundane answer is that I discovered I like using a typewriter. There is a certain pleasure in it, like rediscovering the joy of vinyl records after the joyless immateriality of music streaming. But there is also a strangely remarkable answer to the question why I have returned to the manual typewriter keyboard, which it is difficult for me to articulate, despite my supposed ability with words. When I write on a typewriter I can feel my brain working differently. Perhaps I can describe the feeling as if a part of me, a limb perhaps, has been folded in one position, and unused for a long time, and now it can move again. Of course it feels a bit stiff and not quite as nimble as it once was, but equally there is a sense of release, perhaps even relief at being able to move again.

That is an attempt to express in words a sensory or aesthetic feeling, and it can only approximate what it is really like. There is much more to it, not least the sense of something that almost resembles a frisson of danger as I press down on the keys, with unarticulated thought passing from my mind to my fingers to the keys. Like cutting wood or stone, to type is to make a permanent mark, in a way that is wholly unlike typing on a word-processor, and the sense that there is no going back on the striking of the keys, except through some other physical intervention, is both terrifying and exhilarating. It would be possible to mitigate by writing out what I intend to type longhand and thentyping the script, rather like one of those lost typing pool secretaries, but that is not how I am writing now. I am composing as I type, except that too is not quite right, as the word 'composing' suggests the ideas I am setting down are pre-determined, and the typewriter merely a tool for setting them down. That is not the case. The words flow, often without me articulating them even to myself in my mind, and seem to appear ad libitum on the page. It is both a mental and a physical experience, writing as a physical and material act.

As I say, it feels to me very different to the act of writing on a computer, where a kind of disembodied experience dominates, and a constant process of editing, cleaning up, improving, takes over, often creating highly-polished prose, but prose that also lacks an essential humanity.

Do I dare to suggest writing on this clattering machine is a kind of carving? Maybe that is a step too far, but it has affinities. The physicality and materiality of the process is one, the tap-tap-tap of keys as they force the hammers to strike the paper is another. Yet another still is the terrifying finality of the mark as a descision is made to strike or not strike the keys. But there is also something else, which might bring the whole process of writing much closer to any craft-based visual practice. It is the sense of letting go, of not being entirely in control of the whole process, and instead letting the process itself dictate the words that are created. No, I don't just mean the process, I mean the material nature of paper, ink and machine, working with me in a strange partnership in which we all contribute to the text being written.

I am pretty sure I have written something on that idea somewhere before, and maybe that is what led me to want to use a typewriter again. I cannot be sure. All I know now is that my fingers hurt from hitting these keys and it is time to end.

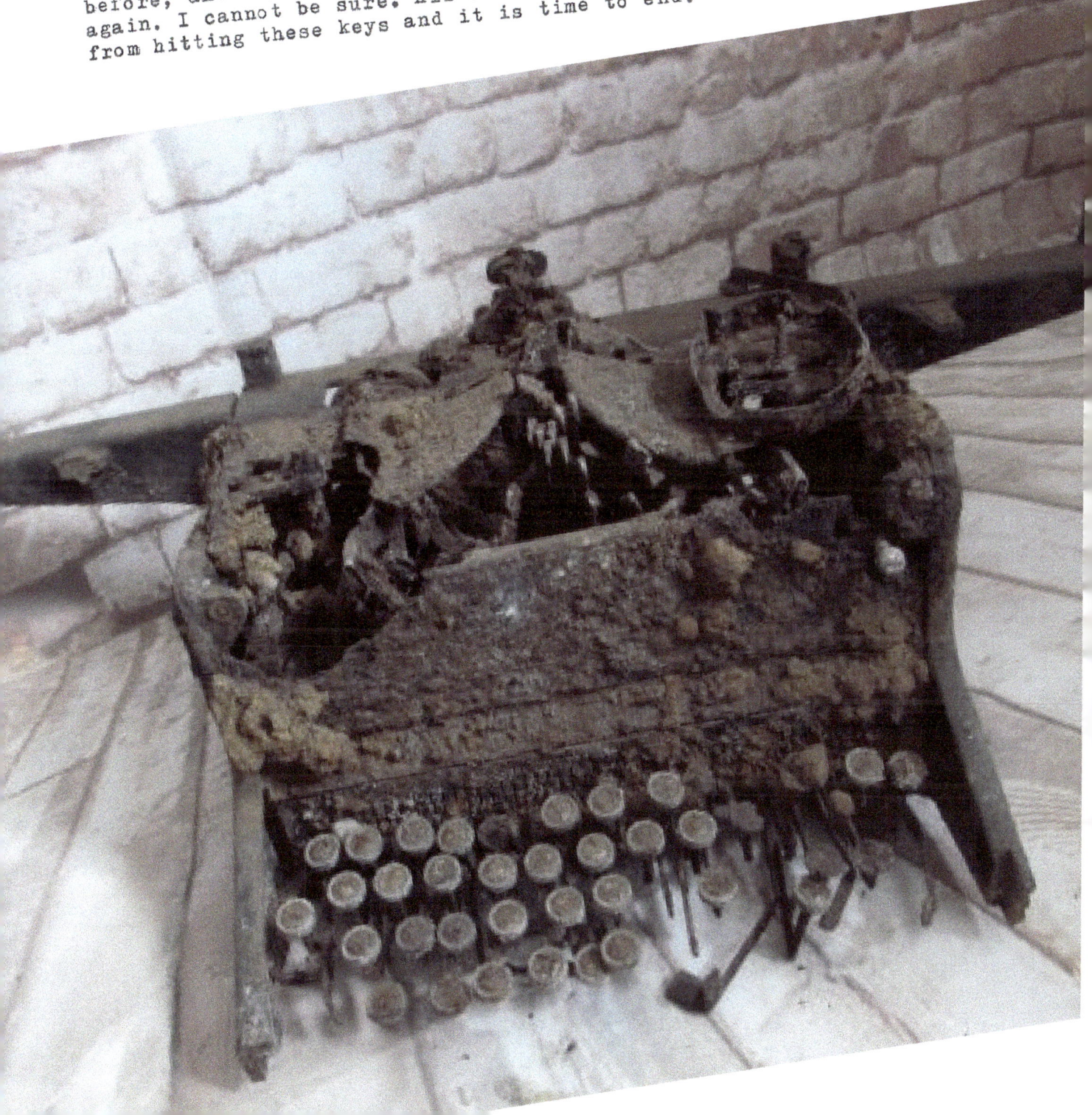

П3 PROVOCATION 3

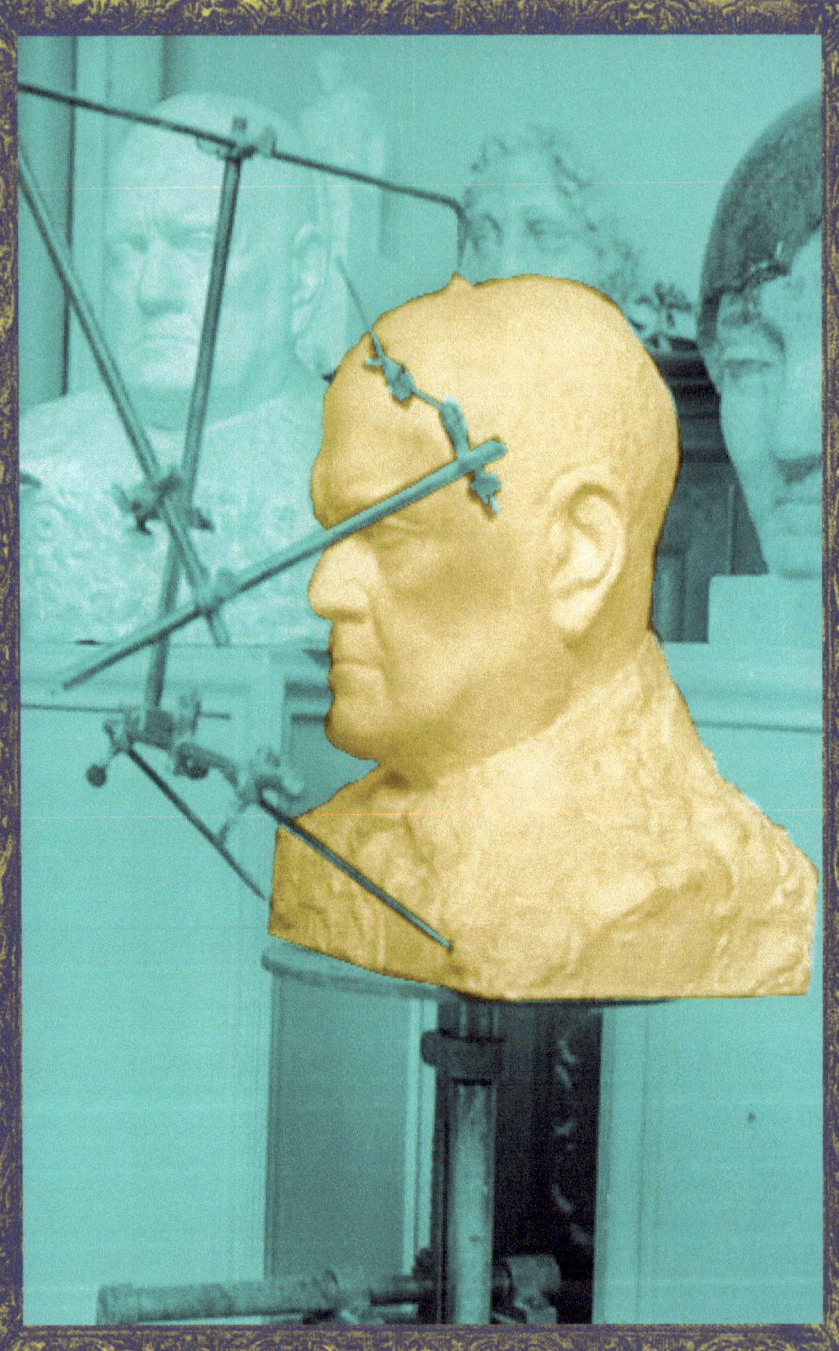

Further Thoughts on Carving
by Matthew Rowe

To carve: the creation of space

Carving is the creation of space where there was solid material. That which is carved is something that:

    (a) before it was carved occupied more space with greater materiality than it does now as a carving
    (b) has replaced material with space, as such replacing material with space
    (c) has transformed what was once a hidden interior into an exposed surface.

Carving is then transformational of the material that has been subject to a carving action. And of the space around the material that has been subject to carving.

A carving: the definition of a space

A carving implies the material before it was carved through the space that surrounds it. However, where once was this was definite and measurable as material, it is now unknown in its particular dimensions as space. There is no way to know where the space around a carving ends; indeed such space, if it ends, may end within the boundaries of the original material.

Carving then exposes both material and space, one definitely, the other indefinitely.

    A question is like the action of carving in how it opens up possibilities that were hidden before. An answer is like a carving in that it sets a response to a question in a definite form.

    If successful, carving is then an interrogative practice. Carving is an act of questioning that seeks to provide material objects as answers.

    So, a carving stands as an answer to a question that has been posed through carving. Thus, we can ask of any carving "What (sort of) question was this trying to answer?" and ask of any activity of carving, 'What kind of answer are you trying to provide?'

    Sometimes an answer can't be found, and this might be due to the question, the questioner or the material or tools with which one addresses the topic. Rubbing a chocolate teapot won't divine tomorrow's weather if you're wearing gloves made of glass.

    Sometimes the question and answer are within the carving itself – a tombstone, a milestone – language carves the answer and implies the question (Who lies here? How far to go?); the space that has been created by the carving is only the lettering itself, and the implied material of the object is very much the same as the actual material of the carved object. Similarly, carving a copy of an existing carving can only provide answers about the carver, not the carving. It is like an exam question in a mathematics paper, to which the answer is already known and which can be done correctly or incorrectly. It's no surprise then that these are both *factual carvings*, semantically, spatially and materially.

    Perhaps then, every other kind of carving activity is less a factual question, and every other kind of carved object less a factual answer, so that instead of questions and answers they deal in hypotheses and responses. So, these acts of carving pose 'What if … ?' through the creation of space, whilst these carved objects respond 'Consider this … ?' materially

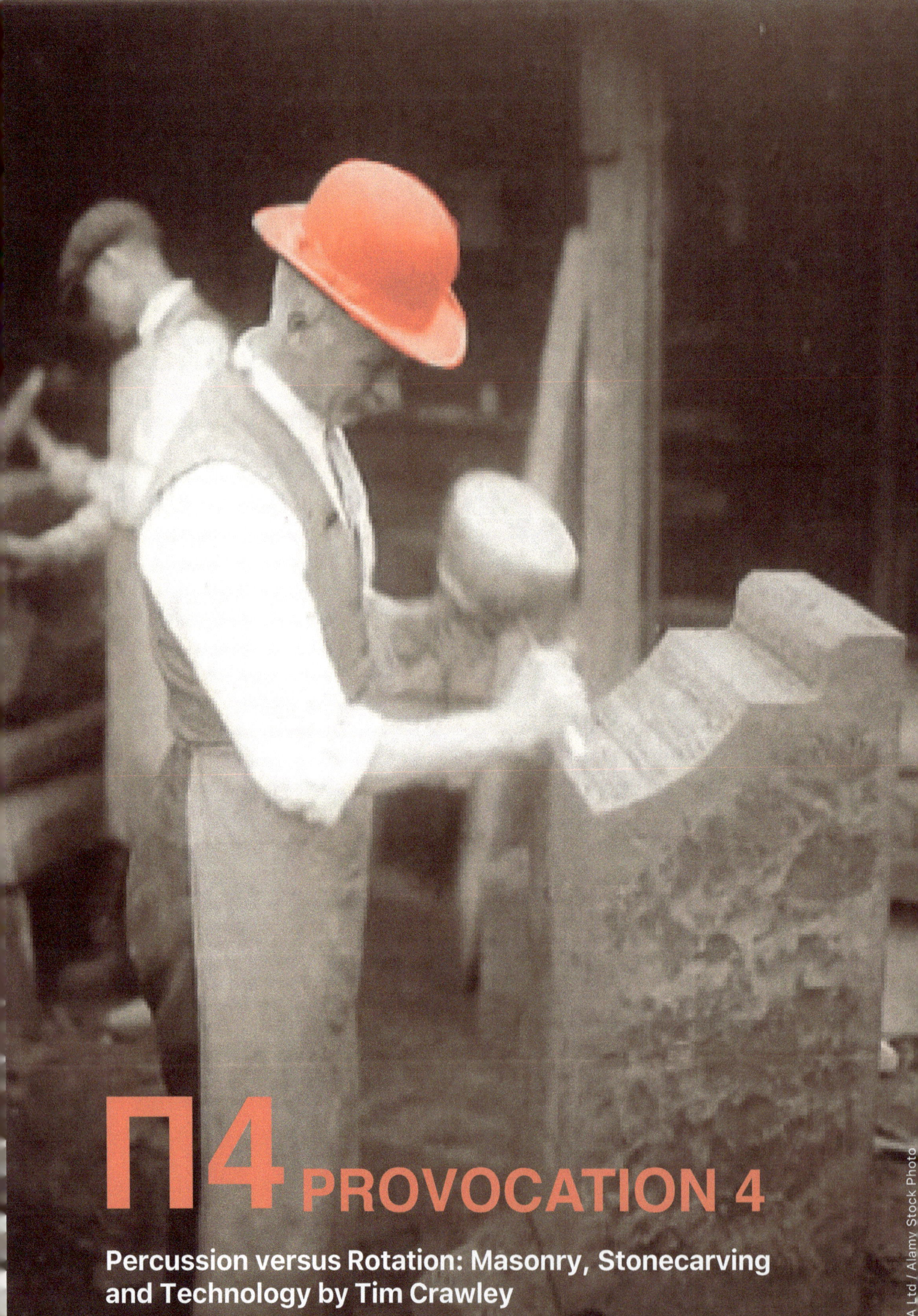

П4 PROVOCATION 4

Percussion versus Rotation: Masonry, Stonecarving and Technology by Tim Crawley

'The past is a foreign country; they do things differently there'

J.P. Hartley

The carving of stone is one of the most ancient of human crafts. Since the Iron Age the tools used have remained essentially unchanged, meaning that this way of working goes back some three millennia and largely survived the Industrial Revolution. However, in the space of the last few decades the craft has been transformed by new technologies. I am a stonecarver with a career in architectural sculpture and building restoration as practised in commercial workshops and over my working life I have witnessed this transformation.

1989

In 1989 I moved from London to Cambridge to start work running the stonecarving workshop of the master builders, Rattee and Kett. The company had a long history, being set up in 1853 following the meeting of the two eponymous founders, both woodcarvers, who met whilst at work on the Houses of Parliament that was under construction at this time. For around a century, the purpose built premises of the company stood proudly at the end of Station Road, between the railway and the centre of town. Through the long windows of the mezzanine woodcarving shop passers by could have glimpsed the carvers at work, positioned here to make maximum use of the natural light at a time when artificial lighting was scarce. Due to its location, Rattee and Kett had a very strong presence in the town. James Rattee, who carved the choir stalls in Ely Cathedral, died young at the age of 35, but the Ketts established something of a dynasty, and George Kett had two terms as mayor. The company rapidly earned a national reputation and worked on many projects for leading architects such as Pugin and Scott.

By 1989 the company workshops had been replaced by office buildings, and the whole operation was centred on another site close by, which had originally been the sidings allowing for the delivery of Portland and Bath stone into the city by rail. The stone banker workshop was in a modern building designed to allow generous natural lighting. Divided into two, the smaller part was for the carvers, the larger for the masons. In the masonry shop there were bankers to either side of a central passageway, with anything up to about 10 or 12 masons working there, depending on what was on the books. When carving was required on a stone the masons would work any moulded detailing, leaving the carved detail boasted for the carvers to complete.

I vividly remember my first impressions of the mason's banker shop upon entering, particularly the rhythmic sound of mallet on chisel. Rattee and Kett were commercial masons, but at this time their working methods remained firmly traditional.

There were concessions to modernity and air lines were provided to allow for pneumatic hammers, but their use was generally frowned upon. The use of hand tools was universal, and some of the older masons would rely entirely on pitchers, points and punches for roughing out. On one memorable occasion a French journeyman worked in the shop, and unsettled everyone with his skilful use of an axe to remove waste, which was a quicker way of working and was remarkably accurate and efficient.

The younger masons' preferred method of removing large areas of waste was to put the workpiece on a barrow and wheel it out to a cutting area outside the workshop to a dust extractor to rib cut and more quickly break out the waste. This was done using carborundum blades on a 12-inch cutter. The central boss securing these blades along with the machine's guard meant that a continuous cut was not possible, so after pitching off the ribbed waste, the workpiece was taken back into the shop, where work with the mallet and chisel resumed.

By keeping the noisy and dusty cutting operations outside of the workshop, a pleasant working environment was maintained inside it, allowing for social and often ribald interaction amongst the masons and apprentices (providing the radio was kept at a reasonable volume).

If a fine ashlar finish was required the piece would be finished by wet rubbing with carbo blocks by hand. These hand working skills had remained essentially unchanged for many centuries.

However, the mechanisation of the masonry trade has been going on since the industrial revolution, and large diamond tipped saws have been on the scene since the late 1920s, used to convert rough quarry block into dimensioned blocks either for ashlar or for further shaping by masons and carvers. Examples of further mechanisation were the lathe and the planing machine, both of which I saw at Rattee and Kett, used respectively for turning columns and balusters, and working straight through runs of moulding. Unlike the saws, these machines were operated by masons, who had passed through the apprenticeship process and consequently had the knowledge and experience of working stone by hand which was an essential prerequisite as these machines needed skill and judgement in their operation.

Whilst the large machines took away much of the hard labour and drudgery of many of the preliminary stages in masonry production, the full range of masonry hand skills was still required for the 'awkward bits', such as internal and external returns, stops, and sinkings, and plenty of other work was unsuitable for mechanisation such as curved tracery work and one off elements. Thus throughout most of the twentieth century in the masonry and carving business there was a balance between mechanisation and hand skills and they co-existed harmoniously together.

The days of large workshops full of skilled masons and carvers working with mallet and chisel are clearly a thing of the past, and will not return. I feel very lucky to have experienced something of this now lost world in my time at Rattee and Kett, and found it to be a humane place of work. I realise with hindsight that it was really the tail end of a dwindling tradition. The tradition was not solely that of hand-working, but also the way of organising skilled craftspeople in a common endeavour, which although driven by the profit motive still allowed for those involved to take great pride in their skills and in a beautifully finished job.

35 years later...

Looking back now, I realise that the ten years that I spent in this workshop from the late 1980s were the turning point for an accelerated evolution of hand masonry skills that has now largely supplanted the traditional techniques which it was such a pleasure to witness when I arrived as the new carver. The speed at which this change occurred is extraordinary, given the longevity of the tradition it was replacing. The seed lay in the use of the hand-held grinders as mentioned above, and two developments in cutting disc design enabled this rapid transformation.

Firstly there was the introduction of diamond technology into the manufacture of the discs, which made them safer to use than the brittle carbo versions, and significantly more durable. Secondly, and most significantly in terms of masonry technique, was the introduction of a depressed centre nut that fixed the blade onto the cutter, allowing for the full surface of the blade to be used to make a continuous cut.

The younger masons soon recognised an opportunity to increase their bonuses as with skilful use of the new equipment they could accurately cut direct to the line of a finished draft. The completion of certain details still required the use of hammer and chisel, but this new method of working was significantly faster. It's no exaggeration to state that these new developments fundamentally transformed contemporary masonry practice.

Could these developments be classified as progress? Certainly, the use of this technology speeded up masonry production, but at what cost to the mason, and to the craft more generally?

Unfortunately, as anyone who has worked this way will know, there are significant downsides. Particularly, there has been a significant deterioration of the quality of the working environment. The noise of the cutters is deafening

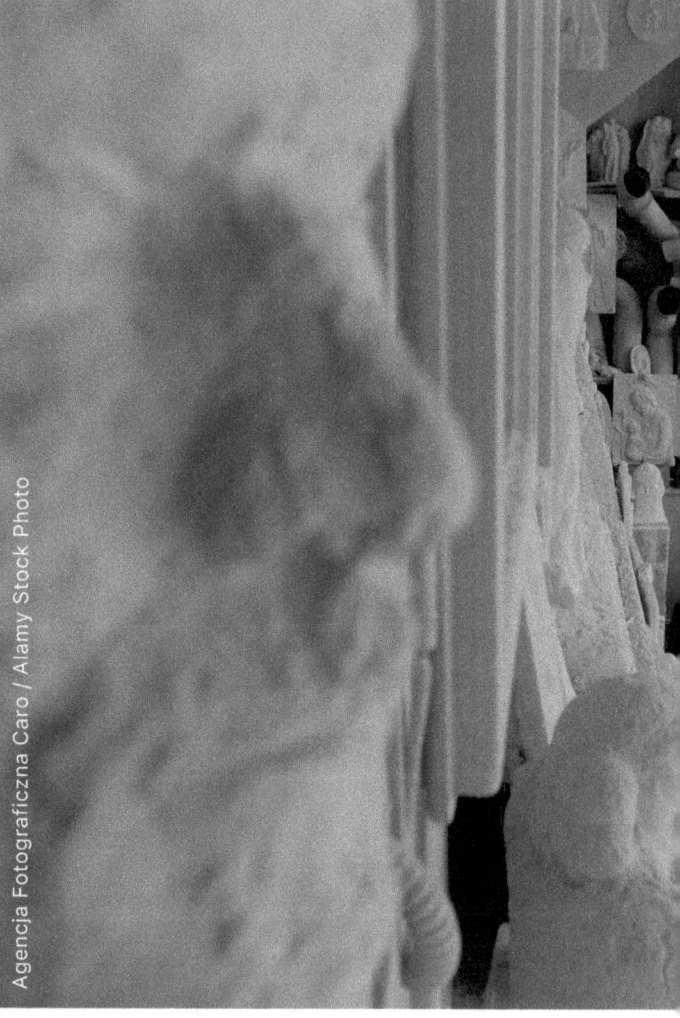

(literally), and they create huge amounts of fine dust, requiring the extensive use of PPE to mitigate the health risks involved. Further deafening noise is created by extractors that contain the dust within the workshop. Ear and eye protection, and heavy duty masks are de rigeur. Gone are the sociable and humane conditions of the traditional banker shop we enjoyed in the 1980s, to be replaced by a hostile environment in which human interaction and communication within the workshop is made next to impossible whilst work is underway. Furthermore, the vibration levels of the cutters have recently been shown to be more severe even than pneumatic hammers, so that extended use over a number of years can lead to circulatory problems in the hands and fingers.

Some masons were prepared to accept all this in order to enlarge their pay packets, but the enhanced bonus payments that originally made this way of working more attractive were quickly adjusted by employers, which meant that masons became compelled to use cutters in order to keep their jobs. However, despite this change in technique, the emphasis remained on the hand

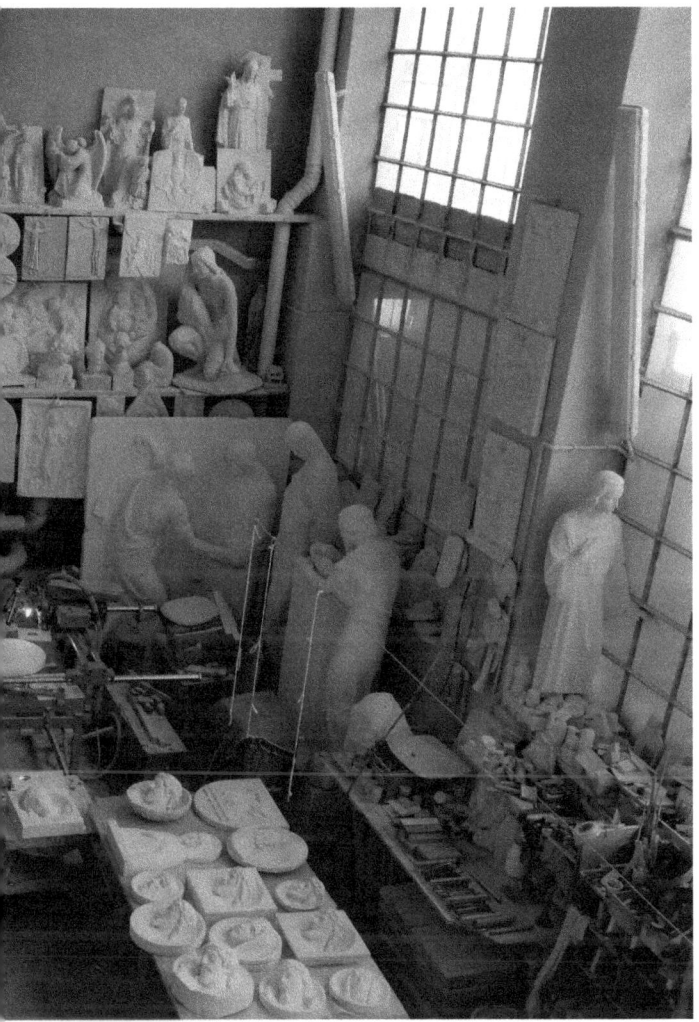

control of the tool, meaning that human skill, judgement and control remained at the key interface between tool and stone.

But concurrently with the advances in the design of hand-held grinders, further developments now fundamentally altered the balance between hand skills and mechanisation in favour of the latter. Again, these developments gathered momentum in the 1980s as a result of the exponential increase in computer processing capacity enabled by the micro-chip. This allowed for ever more complex programming of bridge saws. With the relatively recent addition of milling capacity to these machines using diamond coated milling heads they were able to perform more and more complex operations, formerly only achievable by hand working. Once the skills and knowledge of the experienced mason were indispensable in the masonry industry – nowadays the key skill is an ability to programme the increasingly automated and robotic workforce, a role most commonly performed by the masonry draughtsman. More and more the role of traditional hand skills in masonry production has been marginalised.

I witnessed the transformation of the masonry trade with some misgiving, but complacently felt that the same process could not occur with carving. It's easy to see how the hard data of the masonry setting out drawing can be converted into a programmable sequence of operations that can be performed by a machine, rather than a human being, because the fundamental basis of the craft of masonry is that of plane geometry. Masons' work is directed by the template. In contrast, the fundamental basis of the craft of carving is that of freehand drawing. A carver must learn to visualise a form (ornamental, foliate or figurative) within the solid mass of the stone and to gradually release it through an incrementally subtractive technique that is essentially like drawing in three dimensions.

Surely, I felt, no amount of technology could supplant the human input required in carving?

Further advances in the digital world soon disabused me of this comforting illusion. Again, the increasing speed of processing allowed by the ever more sophisticated and miniaturised micro-chip meant that more and more tasks formerly only possible using human dexterity and judgement could be mechanised and automated. In the carving world, the introduction of multiple axes in milling machines meant that it now became possible to shape complex 3D forms with a router head which could approach the surface from any angle, just like a human carver. Most recently, the development of scanning technology has been allied to the milling process so that it is now possible to mill a completely accurate replica of a human head in marble, for instance, untouched by human hand. Thinking back to the 1980s when I first picked up a hammer and chisel and set out on my journey to become a carver, such things would have seemed the stuff of science fiction.

It is undeniable that in the commercial masonry sector mechanisation has reduced the number of skilled craftsmen needed in the workforce. As a consequence, as the application of current technologies to stone masonry and carving

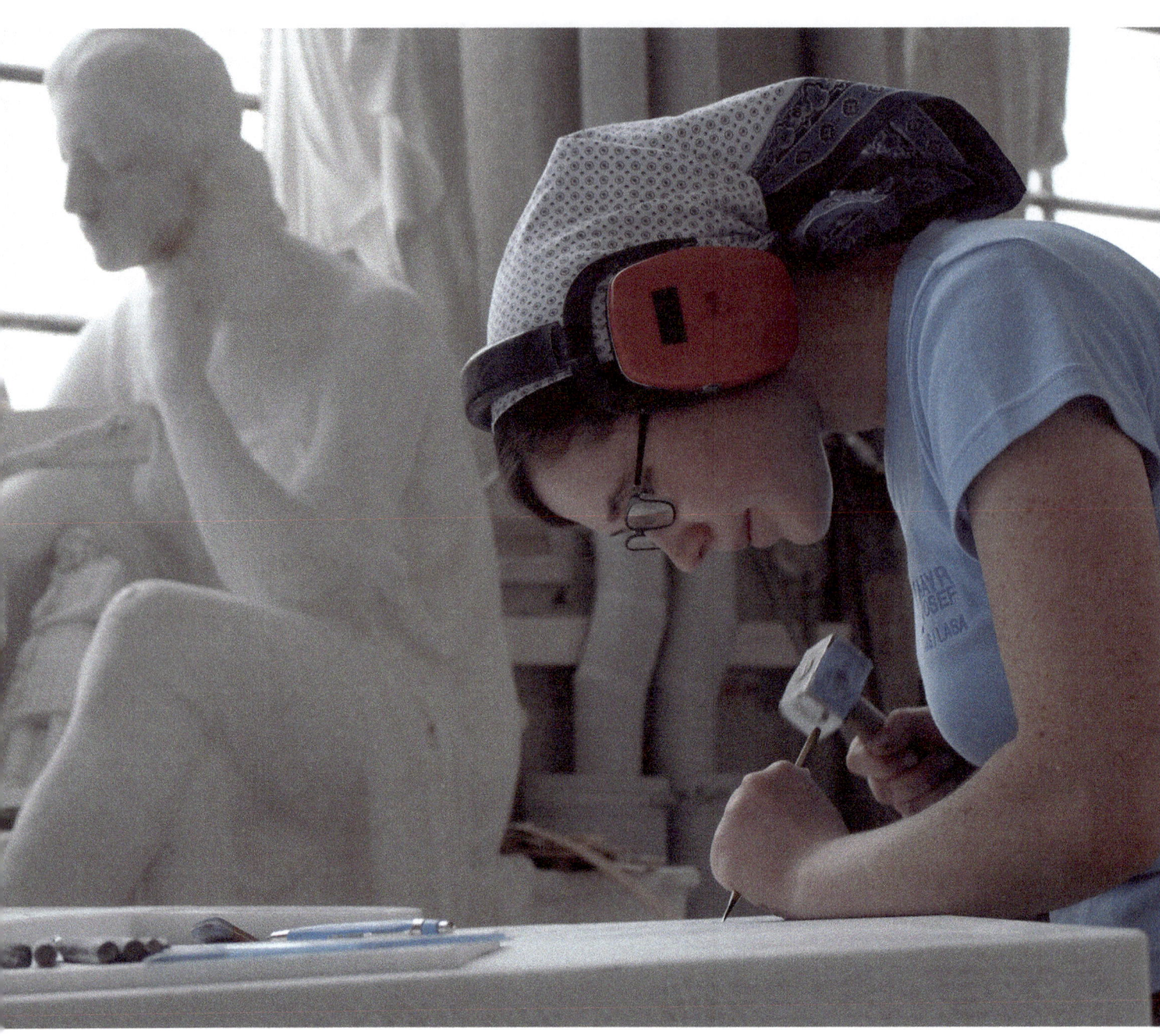

gathers pace, it represents a fundamental threat to their futures as commercial craft skills. Banker masons are now required mainly as finishers. Increasingly, this seems to be the fate in store for carvers also.

Take for example a current project I know of, to produce an elaborate neo-classical building with four porticoes with a full complement of ionic capitals, both column and pilaster, and heavily detailed and deeply carved ornamental urns on the entablatures. When I started my career, carvers and masons would have relished such a project as it would have guaranteed years of continuous work, and paid the wages of a large team of experienced craftspeople demanding the use of the complete range of their skills. In contrast, today, CNC machines are programmed directly from the drawing office so that virtually complete capitals arrive on the bankers ready for finishing, which is the work of maybe one or two days. In the recent past, worked by hand, such a piece would have required perhaps two or three weeks to complete.

For this project, apart from finishing, the only real carving work that remains are the central paterae on the abacus, as the architect has decided to differentiate each capital with a unique design of this feature, which would have entailed too much trouble and time to add to the milling program.

Going forward…

It's not the case that the business of stone working has been completely de-skilled. Techniques may now have changed, but practitioners in the ontemporary stone industry still require high skill levels. The precision and finesse attained in the use of hand held cutters, for instance, is remarkable, and the programming of CNC machines requires extensive knowledge and experience; they don't, yet, operate themselves. Those working in companies using these contemporary technologies take as much pride in their work as anyone in the past.

What has changed is the balance between

mechanisation and hand working, and from my point of view, as an architectural carver who has made a living in the craft, I am dismayed by this. Where will it all end? Will there come a time a time when traditional masonry and carving skills will become largely redundant? In researching for this article I have been shocked to find that this moment is already very much a present reality. The most cursory search online reveals a plethora of information about robotic stone processing.

Take for example a website recording progress on the building of a new Carmelite monastery in Wyoming, USA. Included is a short video titled *Carving a Gothic Finial:*

www.tiny.cc/carmelite

It starts with a description of the digital architectural drawing detailing the new chapel, then leads into the design and production of a new finial. Its design is 3d modelled on the screen, and this process is described by the lay brother, who talks cogently about the design intention and what he is trying to achieve. When he talks about 'digging in deep to create contrasts of light and shade and trying to create a sense of life and movement as the crocket grows out of the moulding' he is describing the process in exactly the same terms as would a carver with mallet and chisel in hand. Another brother goes on to explain how this model is then programmed into the CNC machine, and how tool paths and tool selection are finalised before pressing the start button. The video then concludes by showing the machine in action up to the finishing of the piece. Physical human input into this method of production is minimal.

It is striking how easily the term 'carving' is appropriated by the brothers in their descriptions of their work. What is actually being described is a process of milling, that is the removal of material to achieve a finished form by a grinding process that is rotational. Most readers of this piece won't need to be told that carving is a percussive process in which chisels of various types are pushed through the surface of the stone by the action of a hammer or mallet, directed by the human hand.

Many lay people as well as many in the stone industry might ask, does this distinction really matter? Aren't the developments I have described above just further steps in an ever evolving and long standing process whereby technology saves time and labour and reduces cost, which is of benefit to us all? After all, the history of carving is to some degree also the history of these technological developments; from flint to copper; from copper to steel; from steel to tungsten; from tungsten to diamond. Each stage of development brought with it new possibilities which expanded what could be achieved. Aren't the currently novel computerised techniques simply taking their place in this cycle of change as just another tool at the disposal of the carver?

The challenge to hand working that we are experiencing in the world of stonemasonry and carving has come late to the craft. It has been happening in all areas of industry since the start of the industrial revolution, but since the arrival of the digital era this process has been accelerating exponentially. In the carving and masonry world these technologies are rapidly transforming what has largely been a craft endeavour into a mechanised activity in which the human input into making is minimalised and marginalised. Again, the question may legitimately be asked, does it matter? I believe that it matters a great deal, and that what we are now experiencing in the world of craft stone working is yet another example of how we are sacrificing what makes us human on the altar of profit and efficiency. We risk becoming a race of drones and passive consumers, sedated and controlled by technology and those who own it.

When hand carving stone, the human mind is in charge of the process at the very interface between tool and material. The manipulation of the tool and the hammer through long practice and experience is an almost unconscious action, directed through muscle memory and the communication of eye and brain as the carver focuses on the very point of impact, continually assessing the progression of the intended effect on the stone in real time at the surface of the developing form. There are also other factors at work in this process. The material has a part to play in the way that it will demand a certain way of working, dependent upon its inherent qualities, that will have a pronounced effect on the outcome, and the carver will be very sensitive to this. All of this is the very essence of a craft activity, where the faculty of touch is of supreme significance and will impart a human quality to the work that the human eye is finely attuned to and will immediately recognise.

The milling process described as carving by the monks, in contrast, is entirely mechanical and automatic, directed by digital coding at the stone-tool interface, and is almost oblivious to the material it is engaged with. Human involvement in the physical making has been displaced entirely, and removed to a point earlier in the process, mediated by a screen and taking place in a virtual world where the tactile has no place. The monks have every reason to be proud of their achievements in building their new monastery, but I question the necessity to mechanise the entire operation. Their milling machines will doubtless complete the carvings more quickly than any human carver could, but every crocket will be identical and this will be apparent in the spirit of the building when it is complete.

Computers are quite extraordinary. They can do calculations at the speed of light and perform routine and repetitive actions at speed without getting tired or bored, but at the end of the day are simply adding machines, incapable of independent creative thought and not possessing sentience. Computers also have an on and off switch, and as intelligent and sentient human beings I think we need to be taking stock and thinking hard about using this switch more often and rebalancing the relationship between mechanisation, computerisation and human endeavour.

It is unrealistic to imagine that it may be possible to halt or reverse the march of technology in the stone world, so it is essential that we recognise and champion the value of the human touch and find a way to preserve old skills alongside the new as an expression of our Intangible Cultural Heritage. There's plenty that can and is being done in support of this aspiration, both nationally and internationally, by groups and associations such as the SPAB and the Heritage Crafts Association in the UK, and the World Monuments Fund and Unesco globally. And there's reason for optimism. After all, photography didn't kill painting, the recording industry didn't kill the live performance of music, and the cinema didn't kill theatre.

All of these considerations were summed up extremely succinctly by Nick Park and Merlin Crossingham in discussion in the *Big Issue* about their latest Wallace and Gromit movie, *Vengeance Most Fowl*, watched with

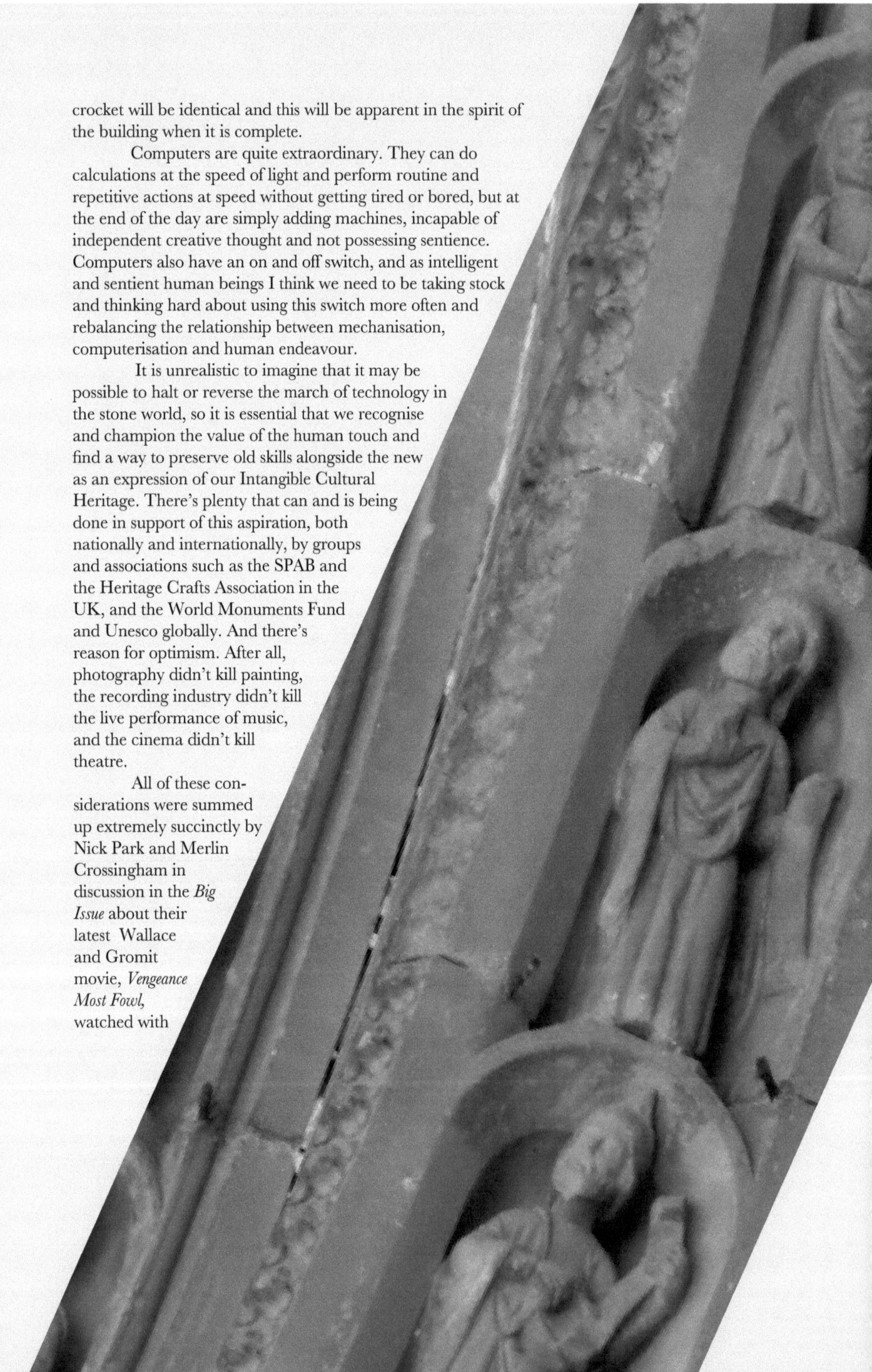

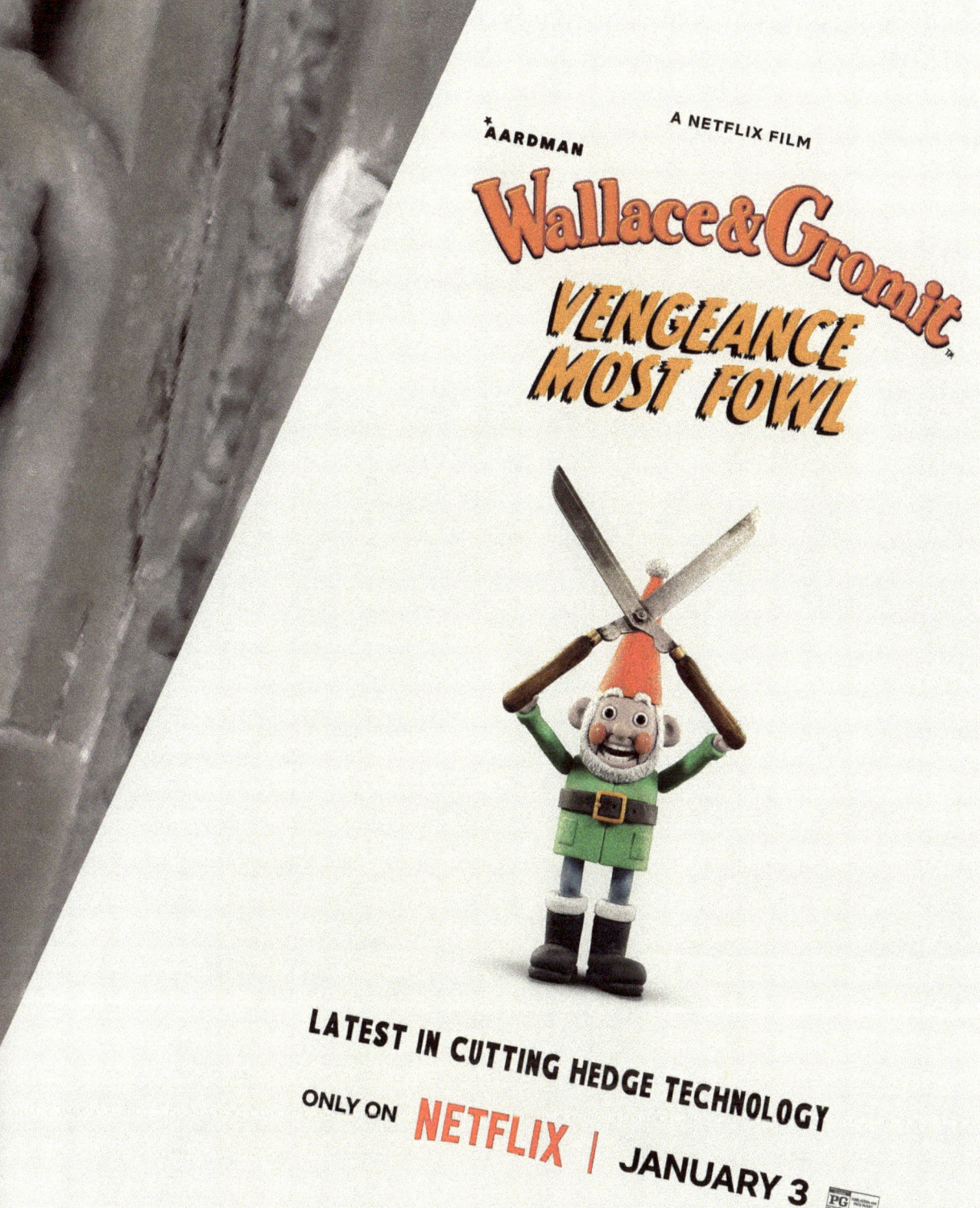

joy by millions on Christmas Day, and the very epitome of hand craftsmanship. They consider the place of AI and the role of technology in relation to Gromit's encounter with these forces in the shape of Norbot, the computerised garden gnome who reshapes his garden.

'Thematically, the film is about… balance', Crossingham says. 'We're not saying tech is bad. In fact tech is great in many ways. But Gromit enjoys the process of gardening. It's not about doing things fast.'

Park continues: 'How much does it enhance our humanity, and how much does it take away and diminish our humanity? Gardening is a good thing to do, creating something is a satisfying thing to do, why take that away from human beings?'

That's why the fingerprints are so important, Crossingham adds. 'The little lumps and bumps and the irregularities that come from the human touch are to be embraced.'

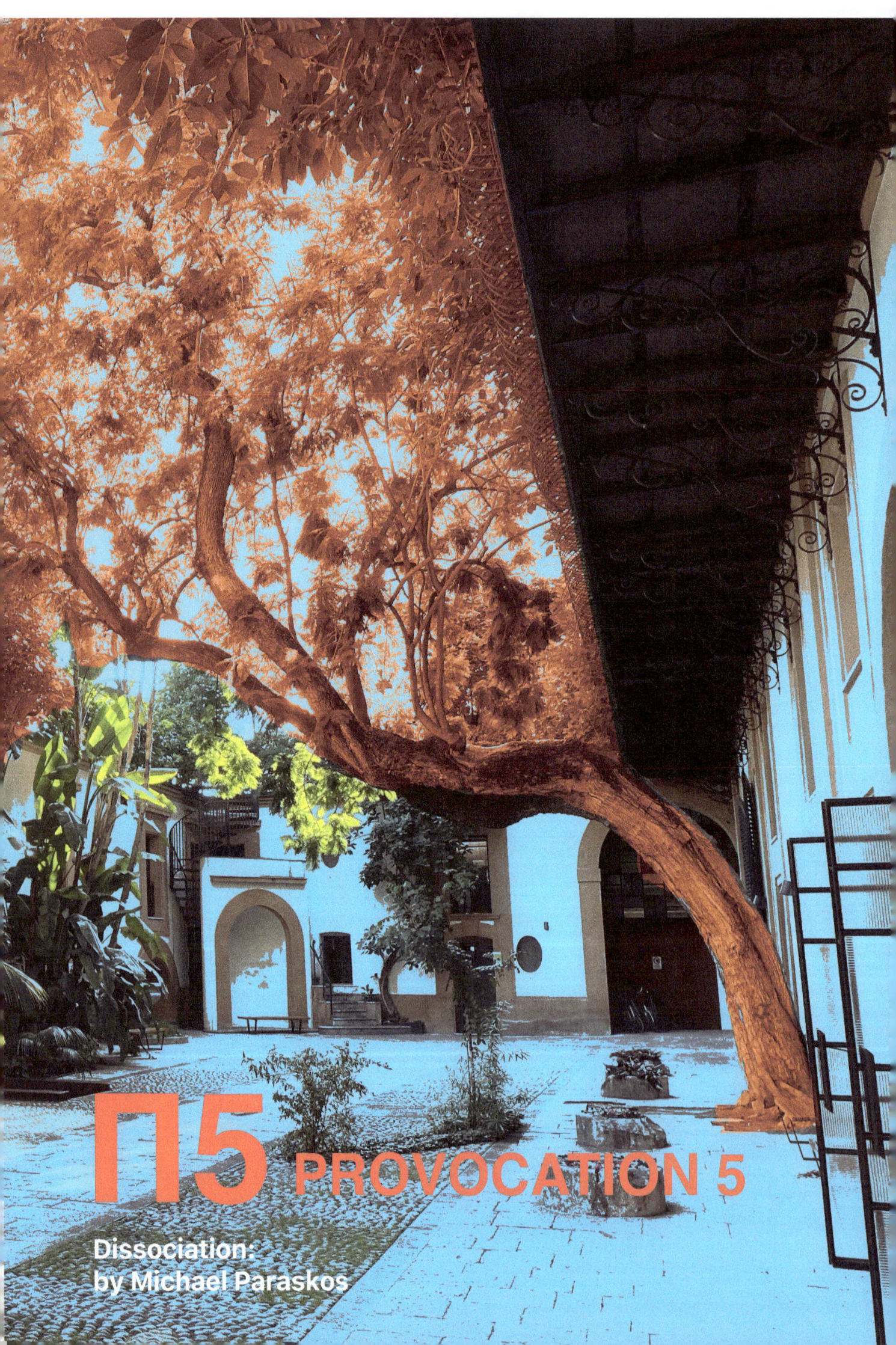

I dreamed of you again last night. Or, rather, I dreamed of your absence. I was back in Leeds, only half recognising the city, unable to remember whether or not you had died. I was too embarrassed to ask anyone who might know, so my thought was to ring you. If you answered, at least I'd know you were alive and we could have coffee together in the Parkinson Court.

I called your old office number and someone answered. I asked for you. For a moment it sounded like you, but the voice told me its name. It was not one I recognised, but it was polite and friendly. I pretended I had the wrong number, woke from my dream and began to cry. It's over eight years now. Shouldn't I be over it by now?

You would have probably joined me in Palermo. It was that kind of trip and all those mediaeval mosaics would be right up your street. You'd have also liked the Palazzo Butera. It is a beautiful museum, full of beautiful things. Unsurprisingly, its owner showed little inclination to talk to me, although, had you been with me, I suspect he would have recognised in your shabby gravitas someone worth talking to. Even my obsequiousness in praising him for his remarkable collection of nineteenth-century English decorative arts objects couldn't stand in for that. But at least I could enjoy, *solus*, seeing work by some of the greatest names in English design from one of my favourite periods. For someone living in London, to be alone in a museum or gallery is a rare luxury these days, making what Wilfred Bion called the 'emotional storm' of other people an inescapable part of the art experience for almost all but the very wealthy.[1]

Despite your death, on my return I decide to send you what I have written so far. Your views still matter to me. I tell you it is about carving. Later that day we meet at the best coffeeshop in West Norwood, the Pintadera, and we sit at our usual table. The Pintadera is unusually quiet today, not even the usual Italian music playing, which gives the deserted cafe an unnerving feel, as though we are trespassers on time. I ask what you think of the text and you say you like it. You always start by saying you like what I write so I am used to waiting for your follow-on comment to gauge what you really think. You ask whether it is really about carving. I say of course it's about carving. *No, scrap that.* Instead I say I think it is about carving. *Yes, that's it.* I say I think it is about carving. *Better not to be too definite.* I say I think it is an act of carving history. Until now all we have had is the history of art and we have tried to apply it to the history of carving as best we could. But for carving the history of art is an ill-fitting suit. Too often it lacks materiality. It misunderstands embodiment. It is too obsessed with meaning rather than substance. So carving historians have to experiment with new forms until we have found out what the history of carving looks like. Maybe the experiments themselves are what carving history looks like. A different way of talking about carving. A wholly different discourse.

You seem to like that, so I add that it's a bit like Griselda refusing to call herself an art historian. You laugh and say you didn't know she did. She said art history was founded on a principle of artistic hierarchy, it is a patriarchal discourse, so you cannot call yourself a feminist art historian because art history is in itself an anti-feminist discourse. It is inescapably patriarchal.[2] Maybe in carving we have the same problem. Maybe art history is inherently antithetical to carving.

Back in Palermo, the ground floor of the Palazzo Butera it is very different to the rooms filled with decorative arts upstairs. Around an open air courtyard, full of mature and exotic-looking trees, is a series of galleries filled with contemporary art. On the walls of the courtyard, set in the open air, are fragments of carved stone sculptures and architectural details. They have been arranged carefully, some on the wall, others in neat piles on the floor. Your absence here feels like a lacuna in my thoughts. I think of Richard Barnes and his Mnemosyne carving project, which combines whole and fragmentary objects with a written text. But the neatness of these fragments in Palermo set against Barnes's description of the havoc of sublunary destruction, is striking.[3] Another dead voice comes to my mind, my father, saying something about this being what bourgeois chaos looks like. Posh! he'd shout, meaning it as an insult. Only later do I discover the organised fragments are the work of two highly celebrated contemporary artists, Anne Poirier and Patrick Poirier, and the objects were found by the builders during the renovation of the Palazzo Butera.

If they are so celebrated, why was that not obvious to you?

The generous answer is that the Palazzo Butera prides itself on not having labels, so you can enjoy the aesthetic experience of the objects without being overawed by the famous names. No Barthesean linguistic signifiers here to anchor you to received wisdom, only the objects themselves, operating as a sensuous relay of aesthetic experience. Most carving works that way, stuck on the outside of an historic building, or decorating the interior of a county house or ancient church, the talented makers left uncelebrated and unknown.

How lovely. You mean they let the work speak for itself and you can make up your own mind?

Not quite. That would be a generous

explanation of the Palazzo Butera, but it's not what it feels like when you're there. For all its displays of decorative art objects and fragments of anonymous ancient carvings, this is still a fine art museum in its ethos and the lack of labels feels like a test designed to separate the cultural in-crowd from the rest of us, the U from the non-U, which is why my aesthetic experience is tinged with the devastating self-doubt that I should know who did this work. A real art lover would know who did this work, because in truth a linguistic anchor is still here, but written in invisible ink so only lemon-eyed sophisticates can see it.

From the courtyard I walk alone into the ground floor galleries. There more fragments, or rather copies of fragments, casts made from a thin papier-maché of Japanese paper of beautifully fragile heads, parts of heads, and whole sculpted figures, lie like ghostly bodies in wooden coffins leaning against the walls. The thin paper catches the details well, but adds its own distresses where the paper folds and the joins show through. You see, they are like Baudrillard's simulcra, imperfect copies. Except they are not simply simulcra. They are things in themselves, and have their own inherent aesthetic meaning aside from the original. Or is that part of the theory of simulcra?

I should know that. Why don't I know? How can I explain all this to my students if I don't know? What should I say to them? The doubt is debilitating.

Just say they look quite pretty, like objects arranged in cabinets in a dusty archaeological museum.

Except this is anything but a dusty museum. It is far too posh, and although these fragments resemble disconnected shards of history, here they have been reconfigured into wholes. Sophisticated artistic wholesomeness.

Sitting in the Pintadera, I might say to you that as I stood in the museum I couldn't help thinking that what I was looking for had something to do with a dialectical difference between wholeness and fragmentation. I thought, maybe the narrative of art has always been about creating something whole.

Something complete and immanent. Even when a painting is part of a decorative scheme it is usually framed in some way, self-contained as though it is perfectly happy to sit by itself. Think of all those altarpieces in the National Gallery, none of them seem to care they have been ripped from their original settings. So if the discourse of art is always about wholesomeness, what if the dialectical difference between it and the discourse of carving is that carving is always, in some way, about fragments and fragmentation?

You are silent, so I try again.

Most carving today is about carving fragments. Repair this section of egg and dart, replace this figure or moulding on a voussoir, replicate this corner of a frame. All fragments. But hasn't the act of carving always been about fragmentation? To carve is to fragment the wood or stone to reach the form you want.

You are silent, so I try again.

Carving has always been about fragmenting the material, but historically even the finished object was almost always a fragment of the whole. No one person carved Karnak, or the Parthenon, or Chartres Cathedral. Each carver carved only a fragment of the whole. In Grinling Gibbons's work, the carvers also carved only fragments, unindividual pieces to be combined. It was only in the Renaissance that the idea of wholeness took hold in sculpture, so it could join painting as a fine art practice, focussed on the myth of objective wholesomeness. Wholesomeness is to fine art, as fragmentation is to carving. It requires a different mindset. A different discourse.

You always start by saying you like what I write, but you always end the same way. You say, *I'll believe you*, without needing to articulate the mildly cutting follow-on: *Thousand's wouldn't*

---

1. Wilfred Bion, 'Making the Best of a Bad Job', in Wilfred Bion, *Clinical Seminars and Four Papers* (Abingdon, Fleetwood Press, 1987) pp. 1-2
2. Griselda Pollock, *Differencing the Canon: Feminist Desire and the Writing of Art's Histories* (London: Routledge, 1999) pp. 11-12
3. Richard Barnes, *Mnemosyne* (London: Orage Press, 2021)

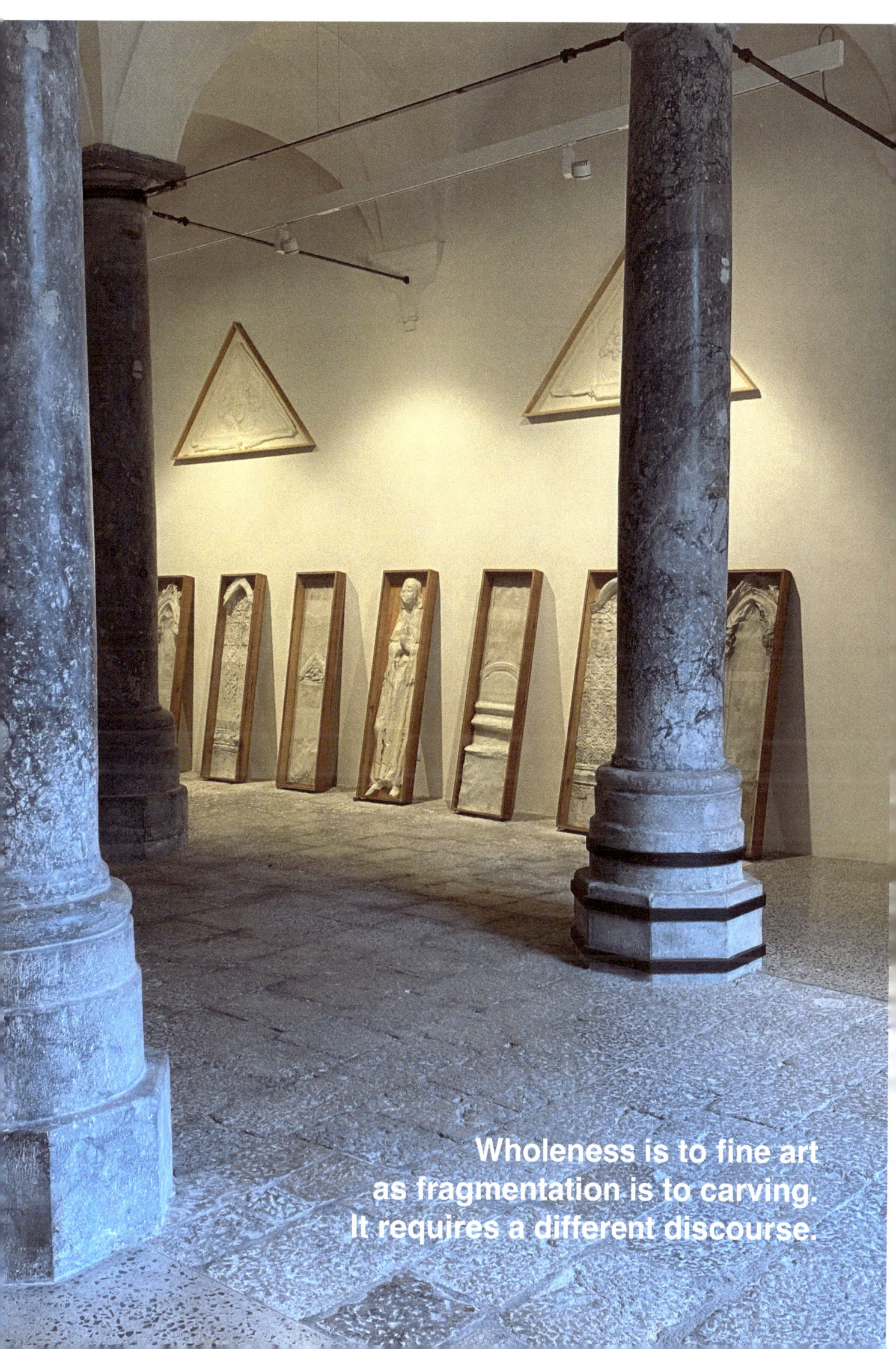

Wholeness is to fine art
as fragmentation is to carving.
It requires a different discourse.

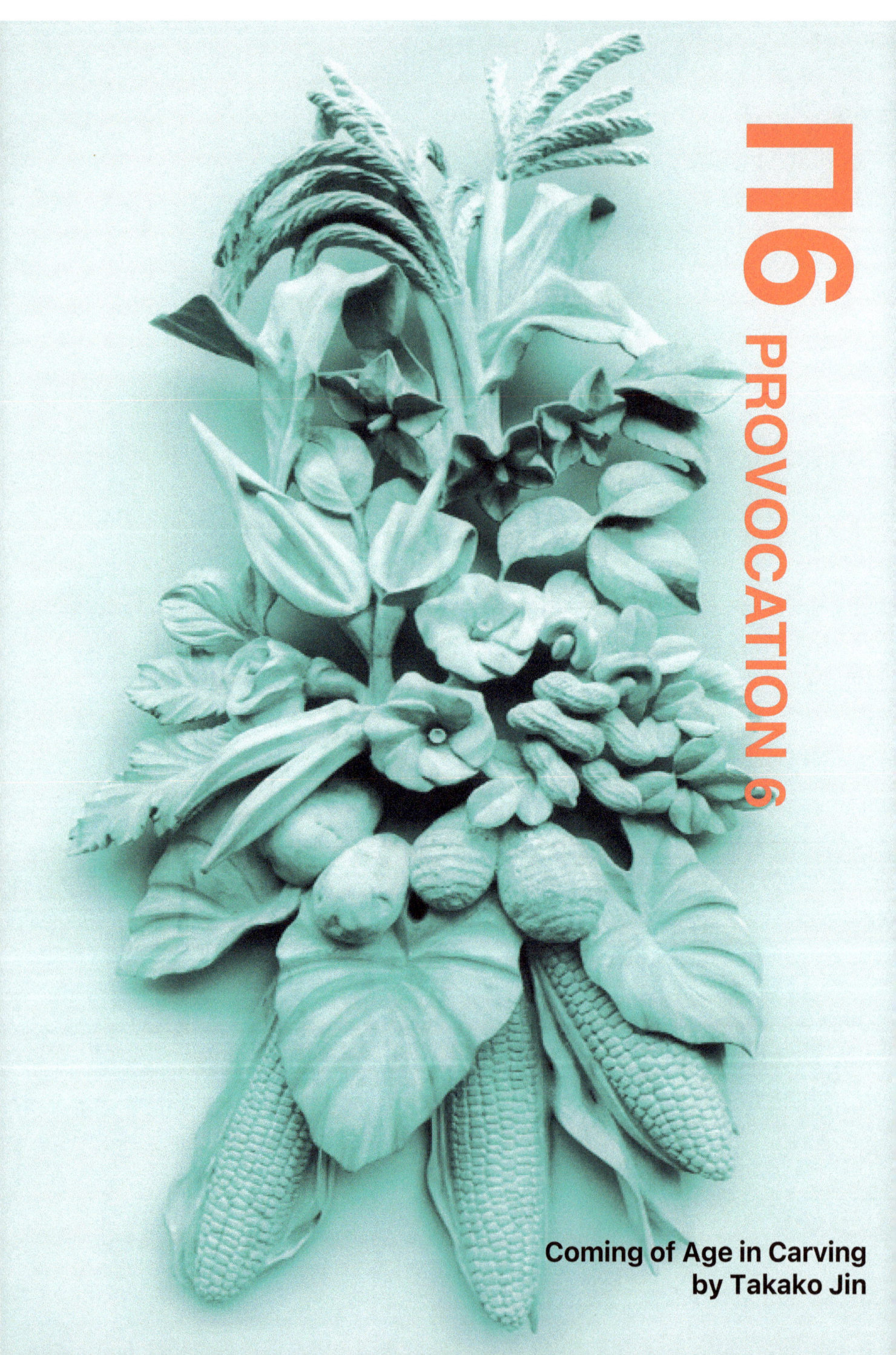

П6 PROVOCATION 6

**Coming of Age in Carving
by Takako Jin**

I have a Japanese colleague that I regularly work with, a seasoned furniture restorer and specialist in decorative surfaces and lacquer work. There is a phrase she likes to use when she is making an assessment of someone's skill-level or ability as a craftsperson. She will declare: "Oh, I can tell they're good, you can tell by their 所作 [shosa]". This Japanese word, shosa, can be translated as behaviour, gesture, conduct or perhaps something like how one carries oneself. What she seems to be suggesting is that a craftsperson's skill is visible in the way they move; that competence is something that is physically embodied.

There are some practices, such as a profession, a religion or even a long-term personal interest, that can become something more for a person than simply something they do. It can become absorbed into their life until it becomes inseparable to their lifestyle, their thought process, their worldview and their identity. In other words, it can become something that is integral to who they are. I have heard people who practice a religion say something like 'Buddhism/Judaism/Islam isn't just a religion, it's a way of life', and there will be many professions that can also alter and shape a person's life and identity in a similar way. They become invested enough in that activity that the boundaries between themselves and the activity they engage in becomes blurred; the activity becomes something intrinsic to the experience of life. Carving, for me, is such an activity.

Traditionally, a young carver would complete their apprenticeship with their master, leave the workshop in which they trained, and spend a period of time, perhaps three, five or even ten years, travelling and working in other workshops. At the completion of this journeyman phase, the carver would set up their own workshop, employ their own apprentices and become a master themselves. In comparison to the historical model of apprentice – journeyman – master, the career path from training to professional development has become less clear and less structured for the present-day carver. In the UK, with the closure of a number of established workshops in recent years, particularly those in the areas of woodcarving and antique furniture restoration, there are now fewer opportunities for early-career carvers to spend a substantial period of time in a professional workshop situation, learning from more experienced practitioners.

My own training and career path have not directly followed the traditional structure of apprentice – journeyman – master, but I feel that there has been a comparable trajectory of learning – development – expertise. After my three years of training at City & Guilds of London Art School, I spent another three years as a self-employed carver, working on all sorts of jobs and commissions, sometimes directly for a client but often for former tutors or for woodcarvers, gilders, conservators and letterers, who were already established in the industry. This was an important phase of development, in which I was exposed to a variety of professional contexts for woodcarving, gilding and restoration, often under the guidance of a more experienced practitioner.

After those first years of self-employment, I was offered a full-time employed position at Carvers & Gilders Ltd, a well-respected London workshop founded in 1978. They specialised in eighteenth-century English giltwood furniture restoration, along with a variety of other related carving, gilding and design work. In my first year there, I was a trainee restorer/conservator, learning the processes of antique giltwood furniture conservation and restoration. I spent a total of six years in the company restoring and occasionally making reproductions of English baroque, rococo and neoclassical furniture. This was an intense period of learning and absorbing, in terms of the technical skills necessary for the restoration of such pieces, but also in relation to the historical, contextual and stylistic knowledge required, as well as the business side of things. After these six years, I left the company to establish my own workshop and business again, as an independent woodcarver.

I was fortunate in certain ways that I had the opportunity to spend a period of time working and learning within the setting of a well-established workshop, and there will inevitably be certain losses resulting from the dissolution of the highly structured and hierarchical system of professional development in carving that we have been witnessing in the last few decades. Hierarchical systems of pedagogy however, while they certainly have their advantages and can be very beneficial, are not the only effective structures for the transmission of knowledge and skill. In its absence, a different and more organic model of development may arise; one that is more peer-orientated, in which early-career carvers will have opportunities to learn from more experienced carvers, but perhaps more on a job-by-job basis. In this new model, learning may happen more through trial and error, experience and experimentation in response to specific demands and challenges of certain jobs, resulting in a variety of original, creative and idiosyncratic solutions and workshop practices. In any case, trial and error, experimentation and finding original ways of solving problems are routine workshop processes beyond a certain skill level, and essential in any kind of creative practice.

I have now been working professionally for eleven years as a woodcarver, and in the related disciplines of gilding, antique restoration and the teaching of these skills. In recent months, I have felt a change, at first subtle but gradually more tangible. While watching myself assessing and discussing a job with a client, and subsequently observing myself at the workbench, moving through all the motions of doing that job, I began to discover the presence of a reservoir of knowledge and skill that had been quietly accumulating inside of me, which I had not been fully aware of until now. Reflecting on the aforementioned trajectory from journeyman to master, I am now wondering if this is an indication that I am coming toward the conclusion of my personal journeyman phase, and entering a new phase of working professionally as a woodcarver.

A week or so after I wrote the previous paragraph, I received an email from the Worshipful Company of Joiners & Ceilers, informing me that they had accepted my application for the Master Craft Certificate for Carving. I find 'Master' a somewhat loaded term, not to mention heavily gendered, and I have certain reservations about calling myself a 'Master Carver'. However, I do feel as though I have reached a point where my level of competence could be called 'expertise', and that a shift in my own perception, and an acknowledgement of a certain level of skill and experience, would be of benefit not only to myself and my business but also in the context of teaching woodcarving.

It has now been fourteen years from the date of writing this article that I began my training in woodcarving at The City & Guilds of London Art School. In that time, many things have changed in my life, and I think it would not be an exaggeration to say that woodcarving has changed my life. There is a popular semi-scientific idea that all the cells in our body are entirely renewed every seven years or so, due to the constant activity of cellular damage, repair and replication. This, apparently, is only partially true, as some cells such as skeletal cells and cerebral neuronal cells are replaced much more slowly throughout our lives and some not at all. However, I enjoy the idea that, having been carving for fourteen years now, I have gone through two complete cycles of full-body cell renewal, and in that process, perhaps carving has now become absorbed into my cells as an integral part of my embodied existence.

Carving has certainly changed me physically, most evidently in my hands. I have a silver ring that a friend gave me in my early twenties, some years before I started carving. I used to wear this ring as a thumb ring, and now the only finger it will comfortably fit on is my little finger. My younger self used to be secretly proud of my slender pianist-fingers, and now in my early forties, my fingers are noticeably thicker and stronger. My two hard-working hands are almost unrecognisable from the ones I once had in my earlier life.

Carving has also changed me in other subtler but perhaps more significant ways. It has

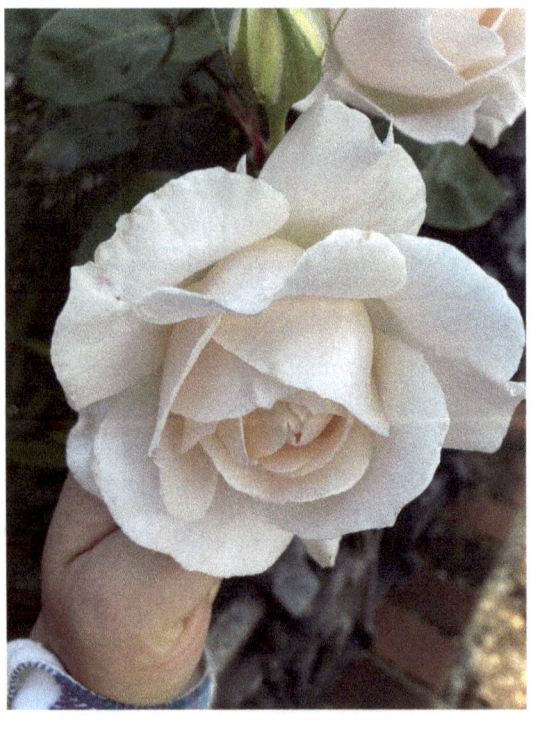
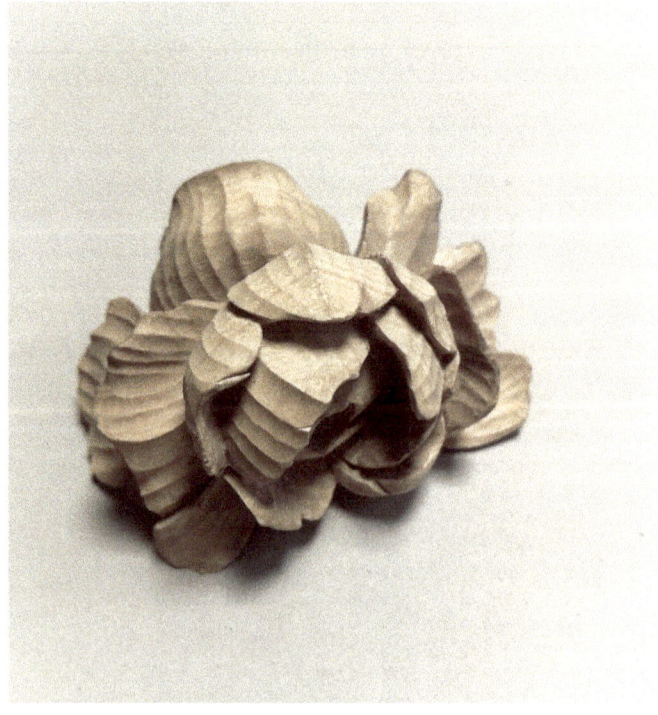

A rose from a neighbour's front garden and a rose I carved in pine in 2019. Image: the author.

changed how I see and understand what I see. Through my training and the integral skills of drawing and modelling, I have 'learned to see', or learned to look, in a way that I would not previously have been able to envision. In that process of learning, I have come to realise the vastness of how much there is to see when we really start looking, and the humility that is required of us to put aside the assumptions we normally project onto an object, and try to see instead what is really there in front of us. Now when I walk down the street and see a rose in someone's front garden, I look at the shapes of its leaves and its petals, the elegance of its forms in all its splendour and infinite detail, and find myself wondering how I could carve it in wood so as to capture some fraction of its exquisite forms.

Carving has changed the way I think, perceive and solve problems. In the initial stages of carving, complex forms must be broken down into simplified shapes. Ignoring the noise of representational form and detail, a carver must initially focus on fundamental structural aspects such as axes and planes. This process of breaking down a complex problem into steps that build methodically toward a level of complexity that can look, in the end, like magic, can be applied to many other endeavours in life. I often now find myself using a similar process of thinking in other things I do, for instance, in the writing of this article. I try to break down the complex process of teasing apart my tangled thoughts into coherently articulated prose into simpler stages; I try to keep sight of the bones of the topic being discussed and regularly remind myself to separate the essential shape of the article from the peripheral details, asking myself whether an idea or embellishment serves to enrich the discussion or whether it is superfluous to it.

Carving has also brought many new relationships into my life, has changed the circles in which I move and operate and, through these relationships, it has changed my perception of my place in the world. I was born in Japan and raised by Japanese parents, but by the age of ten, I had lived in three different countries on three different continents. These multiple relocations in early life undoubtedly gave me some advantages, such as a natural bilingualism and a certain awareness and perspective of the world from a young age. Concurrently, it also left in me a lasting legacy of a sense of not-belonging, despite having now been settled in the UK for more than thirty years. My gradual discovery of my queerness as a teenager in the late 1990s and early 2000s, in a time and environment that offered little visibility and positive representation of queerness, underscored my already established sense of otherness. My sense of belonging in society has been at best shaky throughout my adult life.

It has only been recently that I have begun to realise that I now do have a community in which I belong. This is the community of woodcarvers, stone carvers, gilders, conservators, restorers, joiners and makers with whom I have gradually built professional relationships and friendships, through my years of training and working as a woodcarver. My sense of belonging now also extends beyond my relationships in the present, reaching into the past, through an experience of being connected with the historical tradition of woodcarving. I have been given the knowledge, skills and innovations that have been passed through a long lineage of makers, stretching into the distant past, and I am now in the position of passing on the skills I have received from others, as well as those I have cultivated through my own experiences. It is a privilege to be in this position to teach, to be contributing to the expansion of this community in which we belong through shared skills, shared endeavour and a shared sense of value in the practice of carving. This act of passing knowledge on from the past to the present and into the future not only strengthens my sense of belonging within the carving community in the present, it also creates a larger, more profound sense of belonging within the flow of time, history and tradition.

In these ways, my engagement with the practice of carving has touched and altered many fundamental aspects of my life, and through this gradual process of change, it is almost as though carving has somehow become part of the fabric of my being; as though carving has become absorbed into my sense of who I am within myself and in the world. I am coming to the realisation that the practice of woodcarving has become something — perhaps like a lens or a doorway — that helps me to make sense of my life and the world. It is concurrently a way of making a living; a way of seeing and understanding the world; a way of finding a sense of belonging and a place in society; a way of understanding my own experience of myself as a human being; a way to understand the trajectories of my life including the things I have struggled with; a way to think about what it is to be human in an increasingly artificial and de-humanising era of human history; an activity that has the potential to become a contemplative practice, a way to connect to something beyond myself to something transcendental, perhaps even spiritual.

It is curious how easy it can be to look back on one's journey and focus only on the milestones of achievement or, at other times, the trenches of our failures. The achievements are of course the only

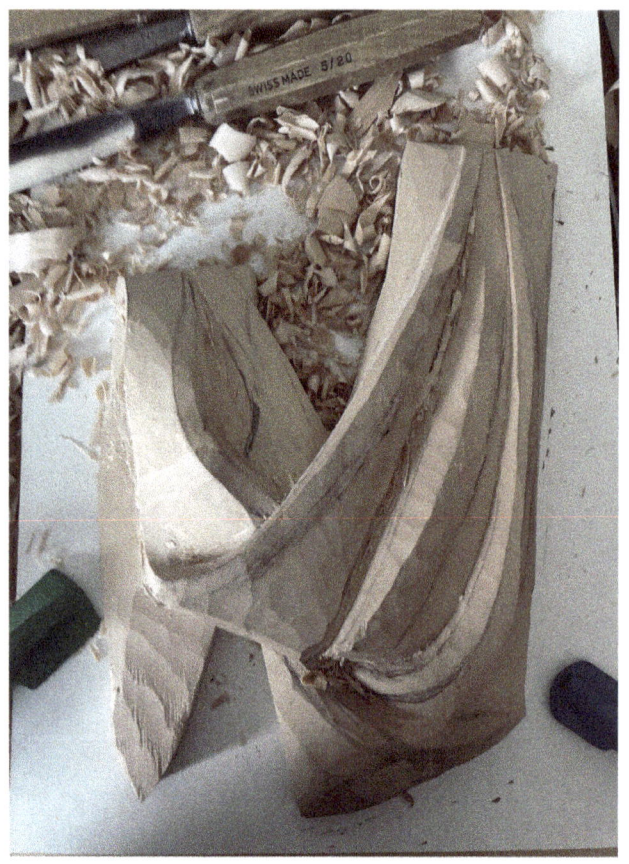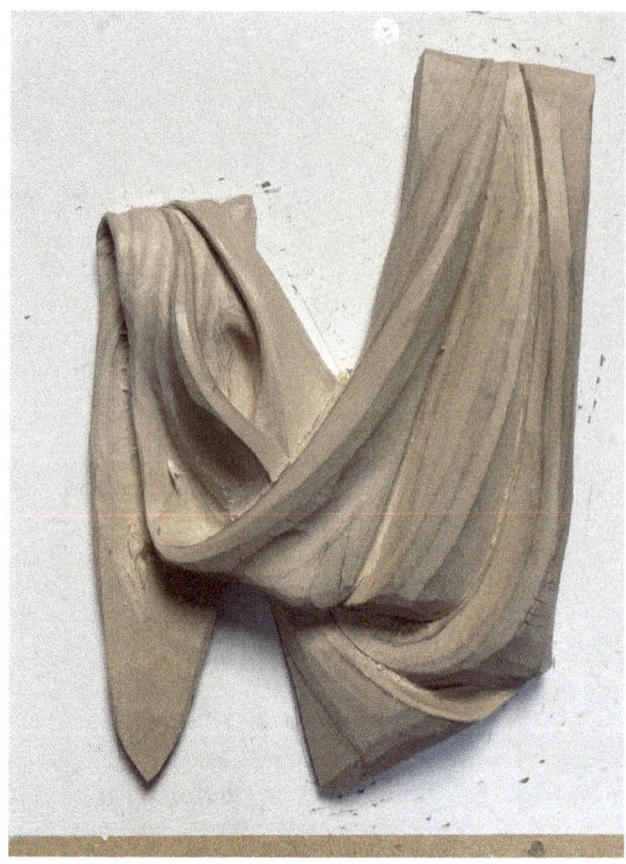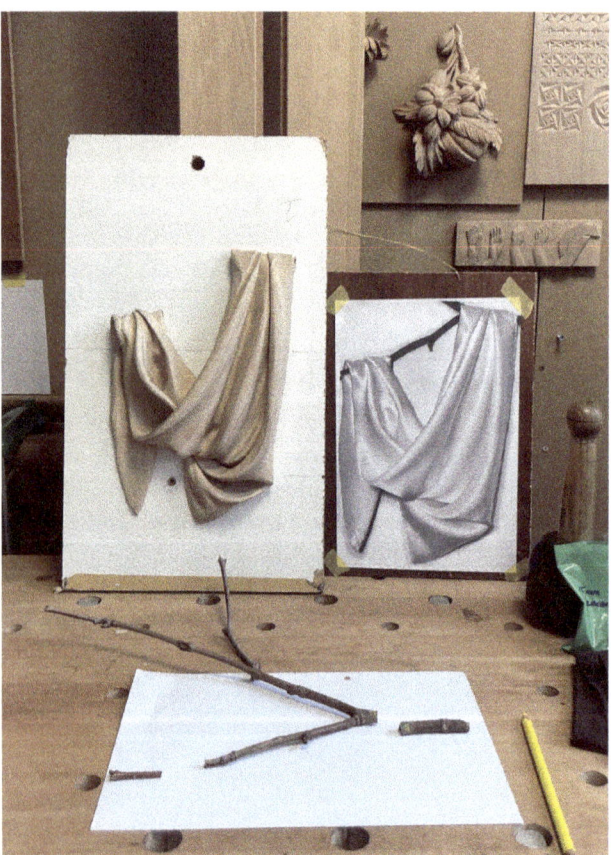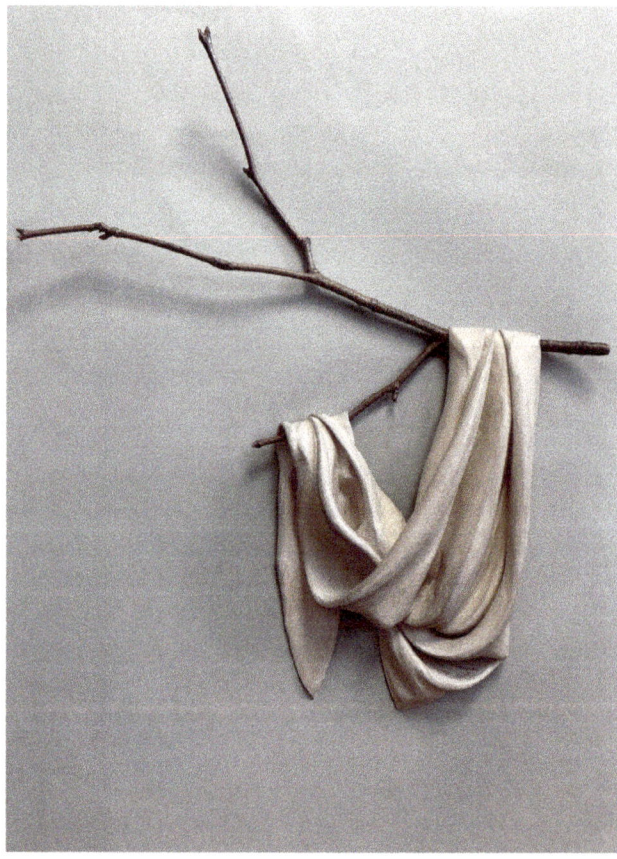

Four stages of carving silk (limewood and a branch 2024 by Takako Jin). Image: the author.

side that people will usually project to the world, especially on social media platforms. It is all too easy to compare ourselves to others and believe that they have more talent, better opportunities, more successes and a rosier career than we do. My own journey so far as a woodcarver has been far from the smooth upward trajectory that I may have inadvertently implied in this article. There have been numerous and sometimes prolonged periods of struggle, even as recently as within the past twelve months, when I have doubted myself and my abilities to the extent that I was unsure of my capability to continue making a living in this line of work. In these periods, the skills and experience that I have worked hard to build up over the years have felt insubstantial and insufficient to hold together my fragile self-belief. During these periods, the engagement and meaning that I had previously found in carving seemed distant and impossible to reach, as if it had been some imaginary landscape I had once dreamt up.

Nevertheless, when I have come through these difficult periods, I have invariably found that time and again, carving was still there waiting for me; my hands still knew what to do with a chisel and a mallet, my eyes could still see the difference between one curve and another subtly slower curve. My hard-won skills had not evaporated into thin air, I had not lost my enthusiasm and wonder for exquisite carvings, and my colleagues, students and friends were still there and still valued my skills and contributions.

These moments of fear will inevitably visit us from time to time, whether in the uncertainties at the beginning of one's career, in fleeting moments of doubt at a tricky stage of a job, over a protracted stretch of time during our careers when the work or the ideas simply seem to dry up, or during prolonged periods of recovery from illness or injury. In these moments, it is useful to remember that our hands and eyes have better memories and are more resilient than our conscious minds sometimes give them credit for. And it may help to remind ourselves that none of us are doing this alone; we did not single-handedly create the tools or the processes we use in carving, nor did any one of us invent from nothing the forms we carve. We have been helped along by many known and unknown hands, both in the present and from the past. It may take a degree of humility to accept this, as it also means acknowledging that our achievements are not all our own. But it also means recognising that no one who carves ever really does so in isolation; no carver is an island.

The journey of the last few months of thinking about what to write for this second issue of *Pygmalion*, and trying to make it into some kind of intelligible piece of writing, has been a surprising one. It has been a process of discovery that has encouraged me to think, reflect and have conversations that have illuminated latent thoughts that have gone unarticulated until now, and has broadened my consciousness of what this thing we call carving might be and what meaning it could hold in our present-day society.

The *Pygmalion* journal, envisioned and realised by art historian, thinker, writer and educator Michael Paraskos, has already stimulated some exciting conversations around carving as a contemporary practice. Despite the *Pygmalion* project being in its infancy, with only one other issue so far published previous to this one, it is fast becoming an incubator for these essential dialogues about carving that are fresh, exciting and relevant, about a craft that has been around since our pre-historic ancestors started to use some kind of tool to shape stone and wood. History and tradition need not be a narrow, rigid and calcified thing that limits and constrains the practice of carving. It can be something that is deeply supportive and connective that acts as a foundation on which a living, breathing, organic growth can happen in the practices, thinking and conversations around carving in our contemporary world.

This kind of growth cannot happen solely in the privacy of one's own mind, or in the solitary act of carving at one's own workbench or banker. It is something to be done with others, in conversations at the workshop, on site, in the café, at the pub; and Pygmalion is also a place where these thoughts and conversations can be publicly aired, pondered, discussed, argued and grown.

I am personally extremely excited about where these discussions will take us and the craft of carving, and what landscapes we might see as we witness the contemporary carving discourse growing up and coming of age.

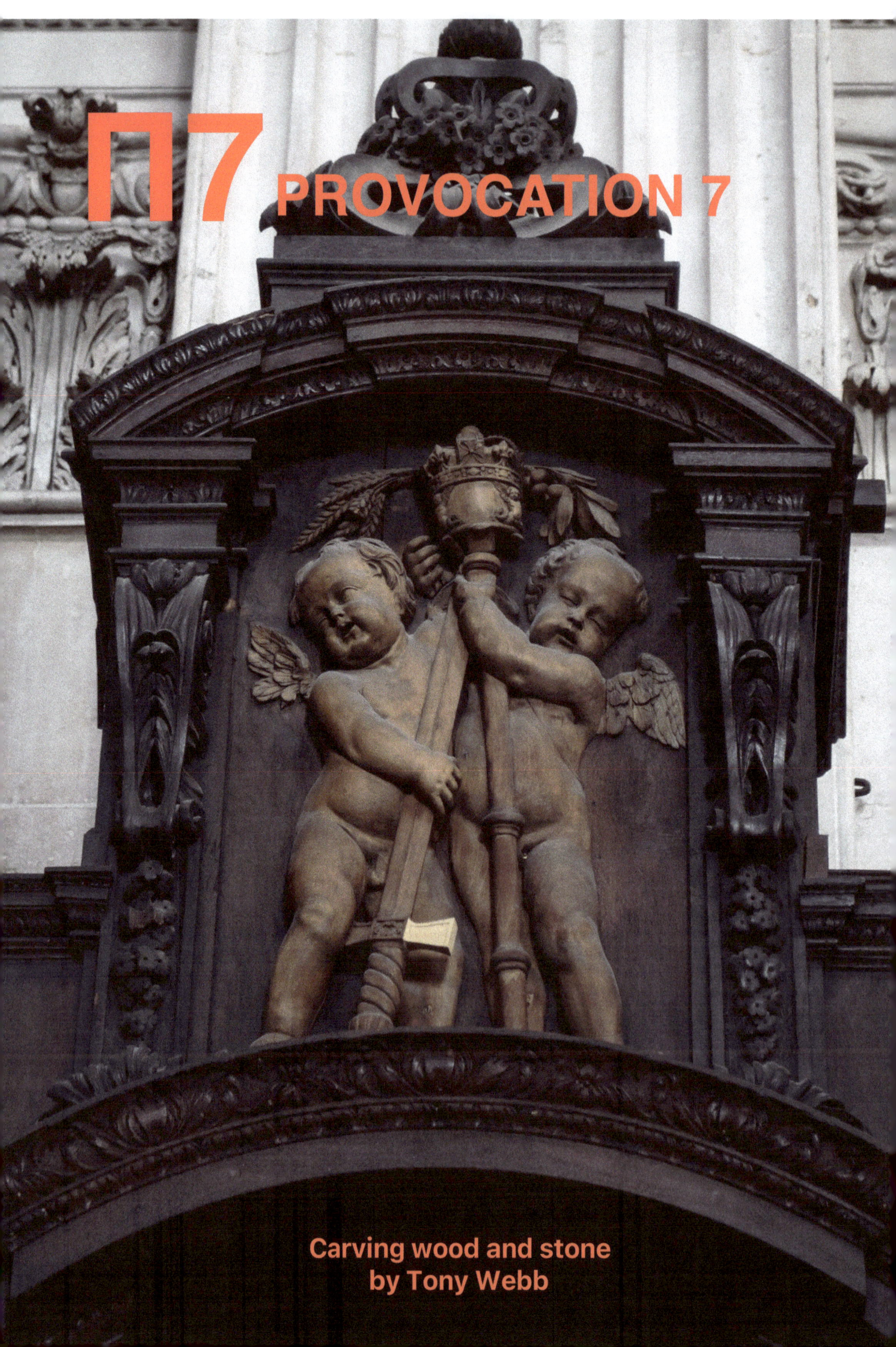

How many architectural carvers do you know who work in stone and wood? Nowadays, not many if any.

When I served my apprenticeship in the studio of E.J. Bradfords in 1952, I would say about 75% of the twenty carvers worked in both materials, and all the five apprentices who were trained while I was there were trained in both wood and stone.

As an apprentice we were given one day a week and two evenings to attend the City and Guilds of London Art School until the age of 18 years, where William Wheeler taught wood and stone carving, as it was the common practice. On my annual visit to City and Guilds show, I always ask why is it no longer the practice and I've yet to get a positive answer. The difference is not that great. Once you have learned to get a 3D image into your head, a few lessons on how to use the tools and you could be on your way.

If you are trained as a woodcarver and want to try stone carving, you need to buy a stone carvers punch and a flat chisel, you can also use old worn down wood carving tools, if you can get one of these very soft stones and give it a try.

If you trained as a stone carver it is not so easy to try woodcarving. You will need to buy a couple of gouges and a block of Lime wood. Then you will have the grain in the wood to deal with.

Do give it a try you might even find you prefer the material that was not your first choice. An old saying used in carving 'A job well fixed down is a job half done'.

I remember clearly during my time at Bradfords when work became slack it was the carvers who only work in one discipline that were the first to go, while the ones who worked in both transferred to the other material. I am talking here about architectural carving as that is the only carving I have experience in and I believe that is where the future is, as stone is eroded away by weather and needs replacing and woodcarving is victim of disastrous fires and woodworm. My training was on the bomb damage of the Second World War which we all pray will never happen again. However it did provide a renaissance in architectural carving. Quite often only just the outer walls of a building were left standing which meant virtually a complete rebuild with the stone carvers going in first carving the stones as the masons fixed them, later the joinery firm would send plain moulding for the woodcarvers together with larger blocks of wood for brackets, cartouches etc.

I must say here that in my day stone carvers and masons were two different trades, and trade unions saw to it that they never crossed. A carver who only works on wood, usually makes a detailed drawing then traces it on to the wood then sets in with chisels to fit the shapes of the drawing, a long and tedious task, which works on small detailed carvings and lengths of mouldings. I have even seen in some cases where the carver cuts the outline shape with a saw, something I find far too restricting. On a larger carving such as a coat of arms it is a complete waste of time. Why spend time tracing on a design then cutting it away?

A carver who works in both materials works in a totally different manner to a carver who works only in wood and I believe a far quicker way.

At a first meeting with a client (usually an architect) I would discuss his plans with some charcoal and chalk, making sketches and adjusting as the discussion progresses as to what he wants. Then if the work is large enough or detailed I would make a clay maquette for their approval, I would then give an estimate of the cost and explain any alterations would cost extra.

I now have a clear idea in my head as to what I am going to carve. No time wasted drawing on the design, or cutting with a saw, you cannot do that with a block of stone so why do it on wood. With my maquette beside me a block of wood the overall size, I begin with a large gouge and a two and half pound hammer wasting away unwanted wood until you see the shapes and forms appear in front of you, in the same way a stone carver does with a punch tool. Look at Michelangelo's unfinished figure carvings and you see the punch tool cuts and the figure emerging from the stone block.

Working in this way you can improve the design as you go along as new and better ideas come to your head. Remember the client is paying for your finished carving not an exact copy of your first drawing. Also if your carving is going in a public place, you will be judged by everyone who sees it.

Should you think that I emphasise too much on speed, that is because I was trained in a studio with other carvers and if you could not keep up with them you where dismissed very quickly. The art is to work efficiently, every tool cut must move the carving forward do not make two cuts when one will do.

I hope by now I have convinced you that a carver who works in both wood and stone has an advantage over a carver who only works in one material.

I have had fifty years of continual work, being paid for what is my passion. Now my passion is to encourage the next generation of carvers.

Π8 PROVOCATION 8

Interview with Jon Isherwood
by Michael Paraskos

MP: It's good to see you again Jon – thank you for agreeing to be interviewed. Maybe we should start by introducing you. You're an artist, a sculptor, and much of your practice is in stonecarving, but maybe we should start at the beginning.

JI: The moment that sort of changed my life, I would say, towards the arts was meeting Henry Moore. It was 1978 and I went to the Henry Moore show at Cartwright Hall in Bradford and met him just by chance. It was an odd moment; I asked him what these things were about that he was displaying. His sculptures, and he gave me two or three minutes of his time indicating that it all came from the study of natural forms. And I was like, how do you get to do that? and he said you must study Art. I didn't really know how to go about that, but he told me to go to Leeds College of Art. I thought okay. I thought that was it, but as someone came bustling over to take him away, he asked them to grab one of the exhibition posters and he signed it and gave it to me. I still have it. It's hung in the office in my studio. I see it as my certificate for change!!

MP: Wow! What an introduction to sculpture.

JI: Yeah. There's always been this sort of constant theme. I mean I've always found great mentors who have helped me find my way, often by accident. I wasn't an artist in school. So, when I went to Leeds I thought I'd study textile design because I figured that would lead to a job. I transferred on to on the foundation course and through the influence of Patrick Oliver I ended up studying sculpture at Canterbury College of Art, where I met an incredible group of professors including your father Stass Paraskos, what an inspiration he was! Then though an introduction from John Gibbons, I found myself working for Sir Anthony Caro in London. I won a fellowship to Syracuse University, and I moved to New York. I thought I would be there for only few years, and I'd be back in the UK, but the odd thing was that I sold three sculptures from my master's exhibition to three American museums, which seemed a little encouraging. So, I thought I should stay around and work. And really from that moment on, it was 1987, the US became my home, and I began a career teaching, running my own studio and managing the US Caro studio three days a week.

MP: But you didn't start with stone carving. You were a welder.

JI: Yeah, exactly. I think that the first material that I laid my hands on was fabric through the textiles program at Leeds college of art., Experiencing the moment when a flat piece of cloth becomes a dimension form, a shirt or pair of trousers is an eye-opening experience for sure. After that I needed something more physical, so I started working with clay and then the clay led to these weird constructions out of cardboard.

By the time I got to Canterbury college of Art which was a truly dynamic sculpture programme. Choices were either wood, clay or it was metal and the artists who were teaching down there were quite influential, leading me to look at sculptures by Picasso, Gonzalez, Caro, Tim Scott, Katherine Gili and all the Greenwich/ Stockwell sculptors who were working in steel. So that seemed like the language to explore, not simulating or emulating them, but working through those visual constructs to find personal expression.

I didn't get to stone until around 1996. In the early 90's I was trying to break away from steel because managing Caro's studio in NY gave me the feeling, I needed to distance myself stylistically and find a material with a great expressive potential. So, I bought some bags of sand and concrete and I started mixing the concrete only using the steel as a kind of armature, trying to get some sort of visceral physicality into the forms. The amazing thing was that the concrete was malleable before it got hard, so you're working it with a trowel to model and form very responsive and expressive surfaces.

The transition into stone came about because of the collector Philip Berman. Phil was from Philadelphia and had a huge art collection including Henry Moore's work. He was visiting George Rickey, a sculptor who made kinetic work. George's studio was quite close to mine and Phil asked George if there were any other artists in the area he should look. George called me and made the introduction. Philip drove up in his fancy Limo, took a quick walk around my studio and said, 'Okay, I'll buy five of these.' And I was like, what? But they're not finished. He tells me, 'That doesn't matter. Finish them and I'll still buy them. But I just couldn't say yes to his offer! After several follow up phone conversations he invited me to his home in Allentown, and there he asked me if I had ever thought of working in stone? He asked if I'd give it a try if he commissioned a piece in stone from me. I said I don't work that way. How would I know what to do? And he just said, why don't you try it and if you like it and I like the results, then I'll buy it from you. And so, it was one

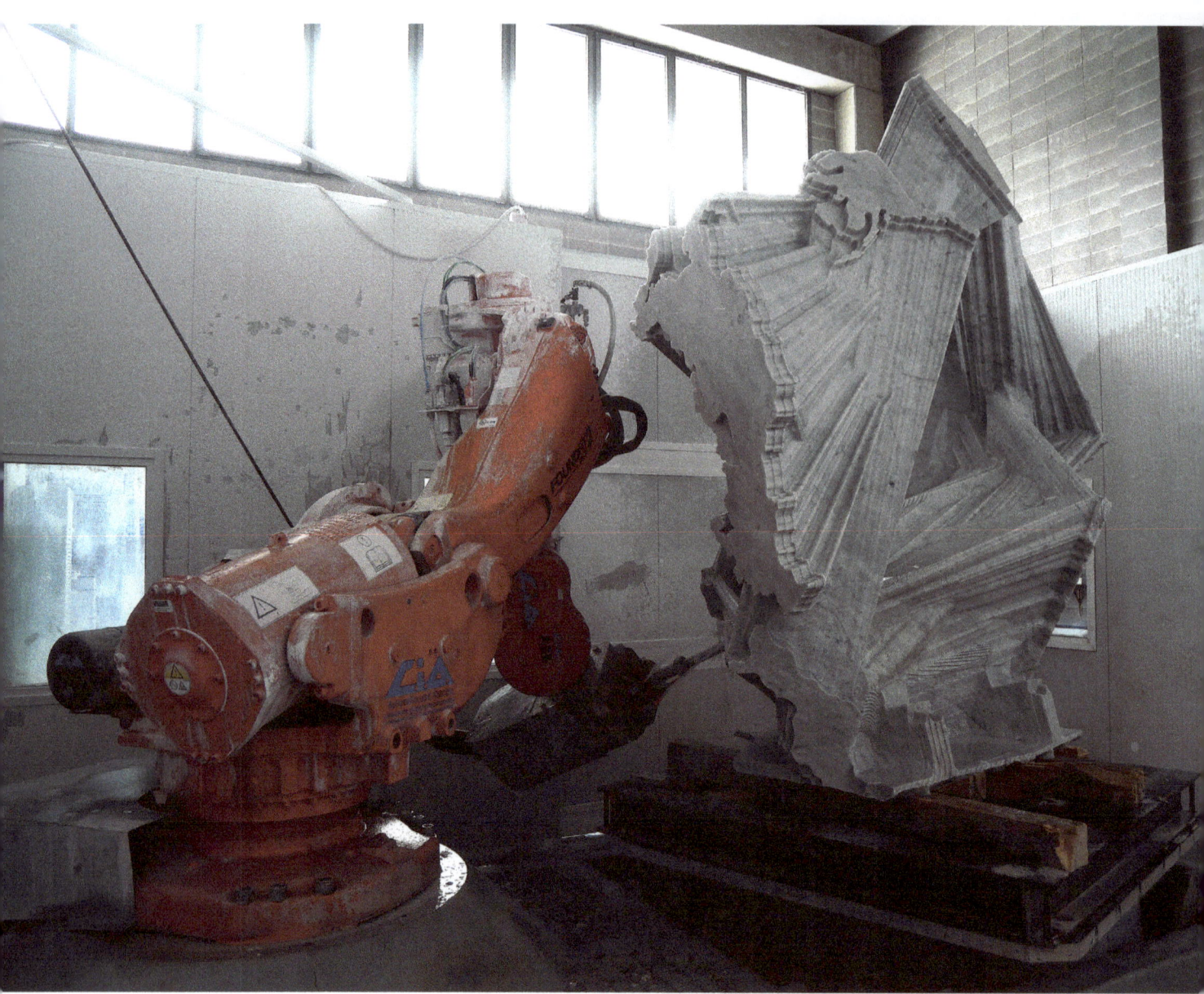

of those accidental meetings that brought great opportunity. And again, a change in the direction of my work.

MP: I'm a great believer in serendipity. So much seems to happen because of accidents. So what did you do?

JI: I did what you do when somebody gives you a new material. You give it a go. I walked up to this lump of granite with the tools I thought I would need, a hammer and chisel, and I hit it. Basically, I just shook from the resilience of the material. I thought this is never going to happen. I'm never going to carve anything with the detail I had experienced in the Greek, Roman and India carvings I admire in the metropolitan museum of fine arts in NY. But interestingly, at the stone yard in Allentown they had a lot of saws and other ways of cutting and removing material. It was mechanical but still quite traditional, pneumatic tools, wire saws, core drills etc. And oddly, in that moment reflecting on the potential to subtract material, made me think of something I experienced in Cyprus. Near the art school in Lempa are the "Tomb of the Kings". I remembered a very profound experience I had of being underground in those tombs, deep excavations into the surface of the earth and feeling this strange emotion. You're in the earth, but you're also in architecture. And it felt like "you're in a body", but its an "out of your own body' experience. So, it was a very complex sort of feeling. I decided what I needed to do was try and simulate that in stone. So, with these huge blocks of granite, I found a way to cut out the interior and make these – I would say – quite emotional works that had these mysterious secret interiors to them. Some you could walk inside; others you could only gaze into.

MP: So how did you end up working with the marble?

JI: The whole thing for marble came a lot later. Along with another sequence of events. I was invited up to Edmonton in Canada to do a workshop. I was fascinated by the fact that many Canadians wore cowboy hats. I was working with a ceramicist, and when he asked me what I wanted to do, I said, I just want to throw some clay on the top of those hats and see what happens. So, we bought a bunch of hats, and we made plaster molds from them. I liked how the molds captured the texture of the weave and the weft. I then climbed up a ladder and I threw clay at them which gave me all these incredible inverted textures and surfaces.

At about the same time I was invited down to the Johnson's Atelier, which is a fine art foundry in New Jersey. They had just established a stone division with all these new carving technologies – CNC milling machines and wire saws. They showed me how it was possible to 3D scan a surface, that you could then turn into an STL file, write tool paths that a CNC machine would follow. So, the first marble pieces I made were translations of the clay hats forms I'd developed in Canada. The whole process really caught my interest! When you think about traditional carving methods for marble and granite. There's a unique quality to stone that no other material has. Specifically, the way it gets finished with the chisel, whether it's a long chisel mark, or it's pointed or it's to a fine polish. It's something you are prompted to consider in the "Slave" series by Michelangelo. The surface handling that supports the emerging forms is often quite rough, yet very purposeful. It's very much a part of the work. It contains these slaves, these struggling forms, but even more so, I like the way that the directional of the tool marks become so significant and powerful. That made me think about how I could use this new technology, whether it's a CNC machine or a robot. It provided opportunity for a new tool-mark. So how do we embrace that tool mark? How do you control the way in which the diamond cutting head marks the surface of the marble. Using three-dimensional modelling programs led to an idea that the machine could give me an opportunity for a new surfacing of marble. And more importantly how that mark relates to the overall form.

MP: How did you get from there to working with the carvers in Carrara?

JI: it was a journey for sure!! As I mentioned it all started at the Johnson's Atelier. Stewart Johnson's was a figurative sculptor, all very realistic, most famous is his somewhat controversial Marilyn Monroe !!!. He was part of the Johnson and Johnson family, so plenty of cash. He'd bought a bunch of CNC machines to explore making his work in marble rather than bronze. I was invited to explore these new technologies, along with a couple of other people. And then suddenly it was announced they were closing the stone division. So, I stepped forward, with three others indicating we'd like to try to acquire the machines. That led to us establishing

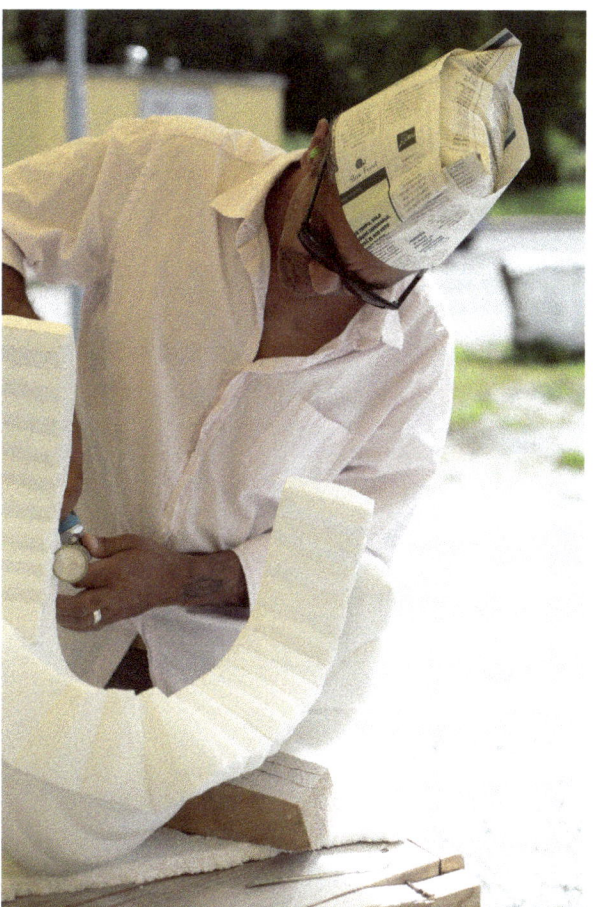

Willam Ranson

the Digital Stone Project, a non-for-profit organization that we ran for about 8 years in the USA provide services for sculptors. So, If you had a project, you could bring it along, pay what it cost to run the equipment and have the assistants help you. But around about 2011 we went through a process of restructuring the organization that sadly ended in its closure. We were all suddenly lost. So I went to Italy, where I always go to buy my material, and sitting in the square in Pietrasanta having a glass of wine with Lawrence Argent and Ricardo Gallenti, reflection on recent events, we decided we should revive the project in Italy. And that's where it all started.

Ricardo indicated he'd take us the next day to meet Stefano Coiai at Garfagnana Innovazione located in the township of Gramolazzo. An hour's drive into the Apuan alps which is the big mountain range that runs along the sea by Carrara and Pietrasanta. Stefano had just been awarded a European Union grant to secure a range CNC equipment to revitalize the stone fabrication industry up in the mountains. We met and within 10 minutes we struck up a relationship. And that was it. That was the moment. That was 2013 and since then we've been running "carving marble with robots" residencies every year.
The Digital stone project is where artists, designers, architects make an application to work with these

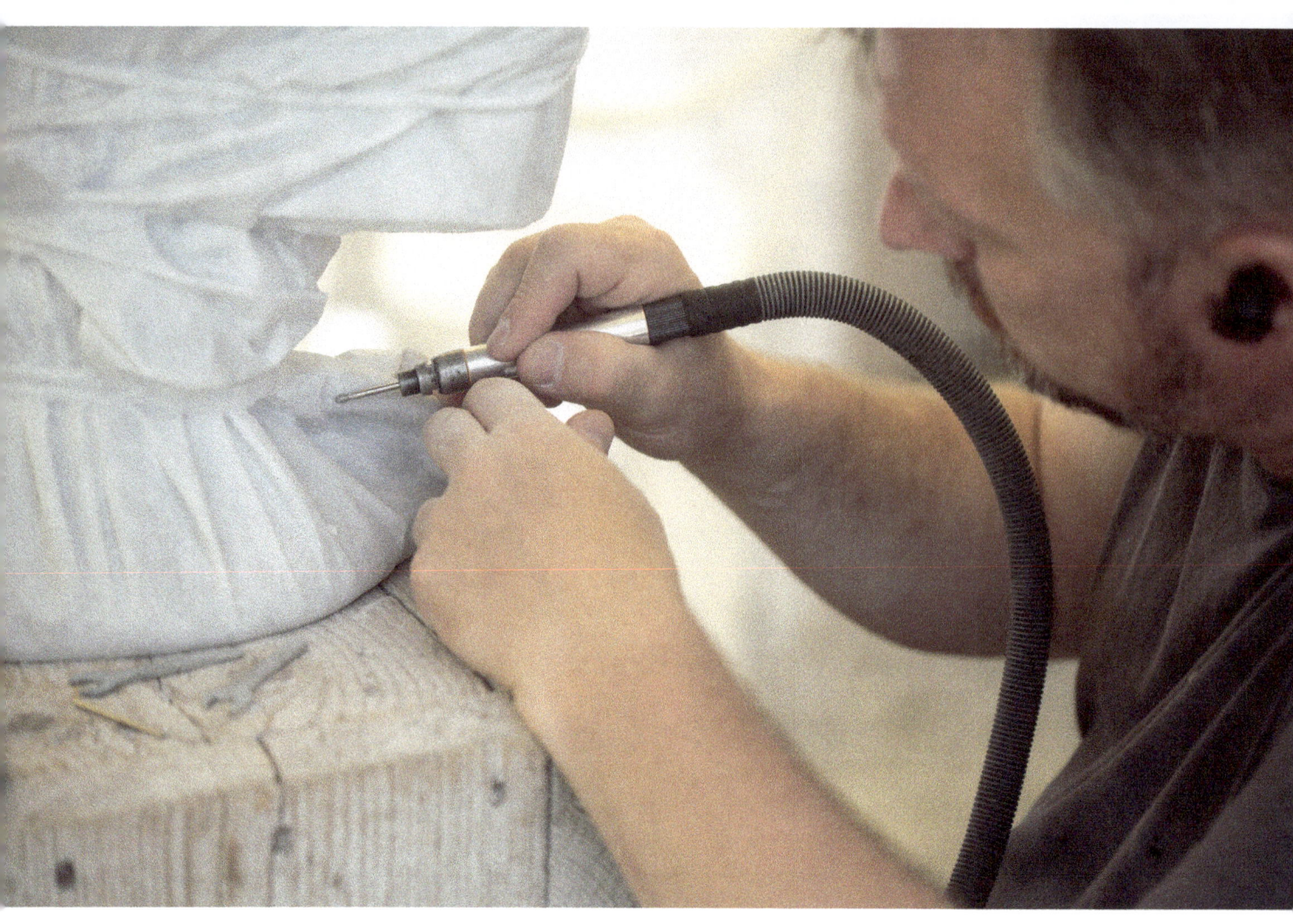

machines. Every year we receive about 30 or 40 applicants. We select about 20 to 25 participants. January through March participants work remotely in dialogue with the technologists who run the robots.
Participants developing STL files, which might be something that's been modelled and then scanned, or that's developed using various 3D CAD modelling programs.

The marble is donated by the four local quarries and what's so spectacular about that region is the wide range of colours available. In preparation for the participants month long residency, their designs are milled out by the CNC machines and then you'll show up in June to hand finish the piece. So, for a month, we set up studio spaces with air grinders and chisels and finishing tools. Additionally trips to Florence, Lucca, art history lecture, quarry tours and the residency culminate in exhibition on the grounds of the Duomo of San Cristoforo, in Barga.

MP: Are they already carvers who come to you, or do you need to teach them the basics of carving.

JI: No it's not a school. I mean, we do have a couple of people who are very proficient stone carvers. *Claudia Dietz*, who trained in Germany –, I think she could carve most things faster than the robot. She's just amazing. And there's a couple of Italian stone carvers who assist in the afternoon, but to your question, if somebody's coming to the residency and its their first time, they get a lot of help. We've had sculptors working figuratively and abstractly, architects who want to explore surface designs, and designers who develop functional objects like tables, chairs and lighting . All disciplines are welcome.

MP: And do you find some of the people are suspicious of all this? I mean, are they there to find out what they might think is the enemy in some way?

JI: Well, that in itself, is interesting. I mean, the robots were embraced to revitalise what was a slowly dying industry. Carving studios were struggling to secure individuals who wanted to train up as carvers. Early on we had an exhibition in Pietrasanta, at the Museum of Sculpture and Architecture, and we got word that some local artists were upset because we were promoting and working with robots, and this was where the craftsmen live, and the robots were taking their jobs. So, we had to meet with the local officials and articulate our process. The traditional carvers and artisans had a point because it potentially does eliminate some of their skill sets. The key issue to understand is that the robot cannot/ doesn't produce a finished carved form ready to be sold or go on display. It can assist in

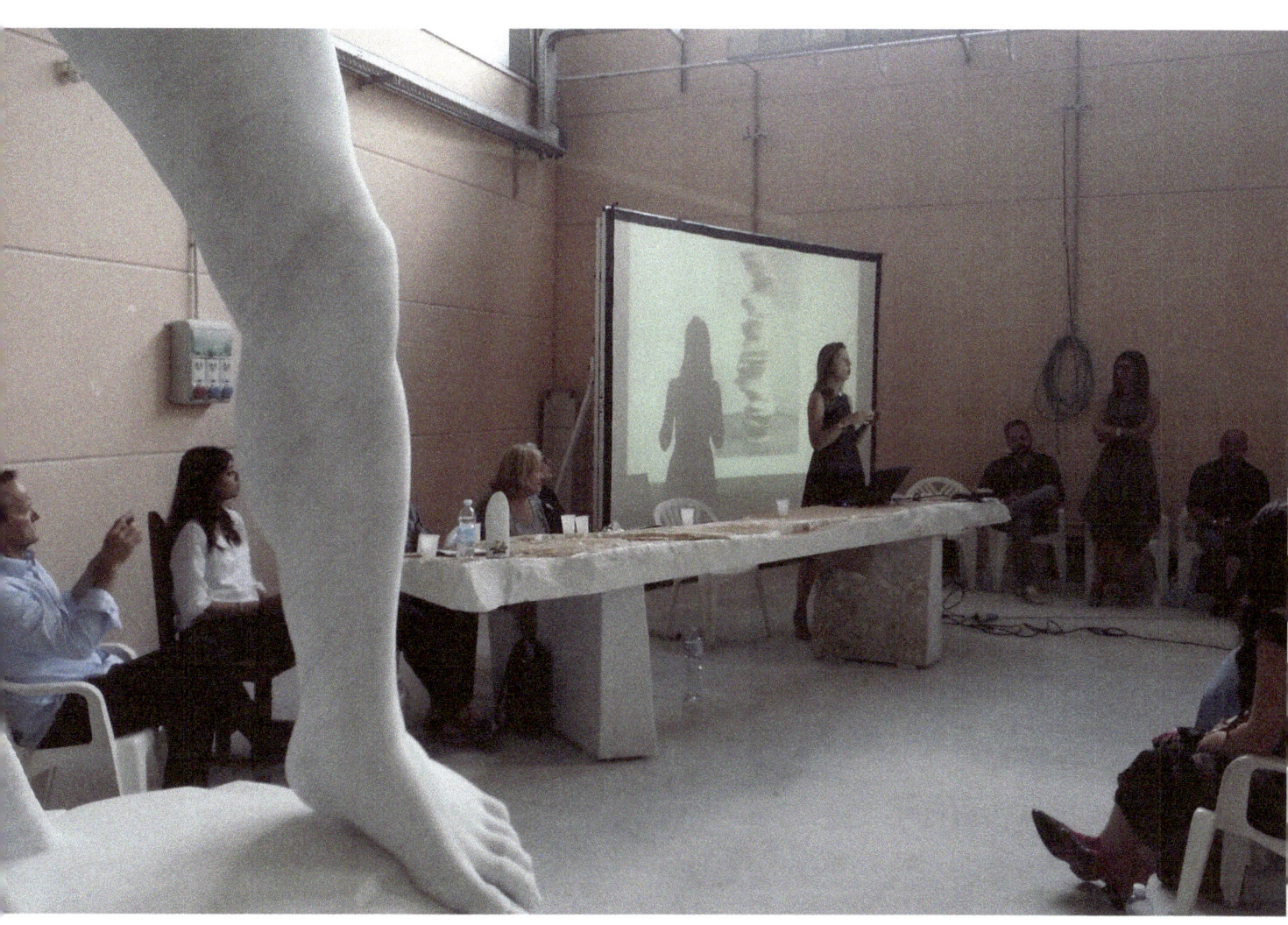

roughing out the form and get in some areas, not all, within millimetres of the final surface. But the carvers and artisans will always be needed to finish the work, bring the hand and expression to the form. Similarly, Chevietti, who runs probably one of the famous stone carving workshops in Pietrasanta – works for the Vatican and a lot of contemporary artists, carving all of these incredible projects – openly shared that some people will indicate they are fine with the robot roughing out the from. And then other commissioning groups will request that its hand carved. So, in one area of the studio, Carvers with the paper hats and hand chisels, big blocks of marble and they're taking a year to rough out the form. And across the workshop there's a robot taking six weeks to rough mill the same thing. In the end the finishing by hand looks the same. I mean, I don't see a difference. But to your question, I haven't noticed the scepticism as much as when we first set up there, about 12 years ago. The robotic technology is clearly integrated.

MP: Given the way fine art sculpture has developed over the past century or so, I wonder whether you think this is just a new carving tool and we're just starting to work out how to use it?

JI: Yeah, I feel that strongly. I am seeing a return to working stone and engage new carving methodologies. It's happening also in architecture and functional design. My experience with this has been that artists are really interested in digital processes. There's a passion for the materiality but very clearly, significant thinking and a desire to engaging with new technologies, AI and CAD design platforms and how new fabrication processes lead to new ways of making forms that we never seen before.

MP: I think that is very interesting. The materiality of using stone seems timeless, passing from the ancient Greeks to the Renaissance, and eventually to Rodin, Hepworth and Moore. That seems stable, but every now and then the tools of carving get reinvented. Iron chisels replaced bronze, and then steel comes in, and then tungsten, and eventually mechanical saws and grinders. So maybe all this is just the start of another reinvention.

JI: You know, I think that there's something very significant in that statement.

I had this show along Broadway NYC Eight sites from Lincoln Centre up to 158th Street. We had to install after midnight with a crane. That went on over three evenings, and in the mornings, I would be there finishing and cleaning up. Amazingly, people would come up to me express their thanks and ask if they could touch the sculptures. They would track the lines I had instructed the robot to carve. When I told them the carving was aided by robots its didn't seem to bother them or when they asked how I came up with the forms and I told them about the integration of animated clay modelled forms and 3D CAD design platforms. They all clearly related to that and thanked me again for bringing a very familiar digital - computer screened world into a tactile reality. My takeaway was that we live in a somewhat virtual world presently with all the media and technology that surrounds us, so, our challenge is to integrate new technologies leading to reinvention for our physical world.

For more information on Jon Isherwood, and the Digital Stone Project, including details on how you can take part, visit:

www.jonsherwood.com
www.digitalstoneproject.com

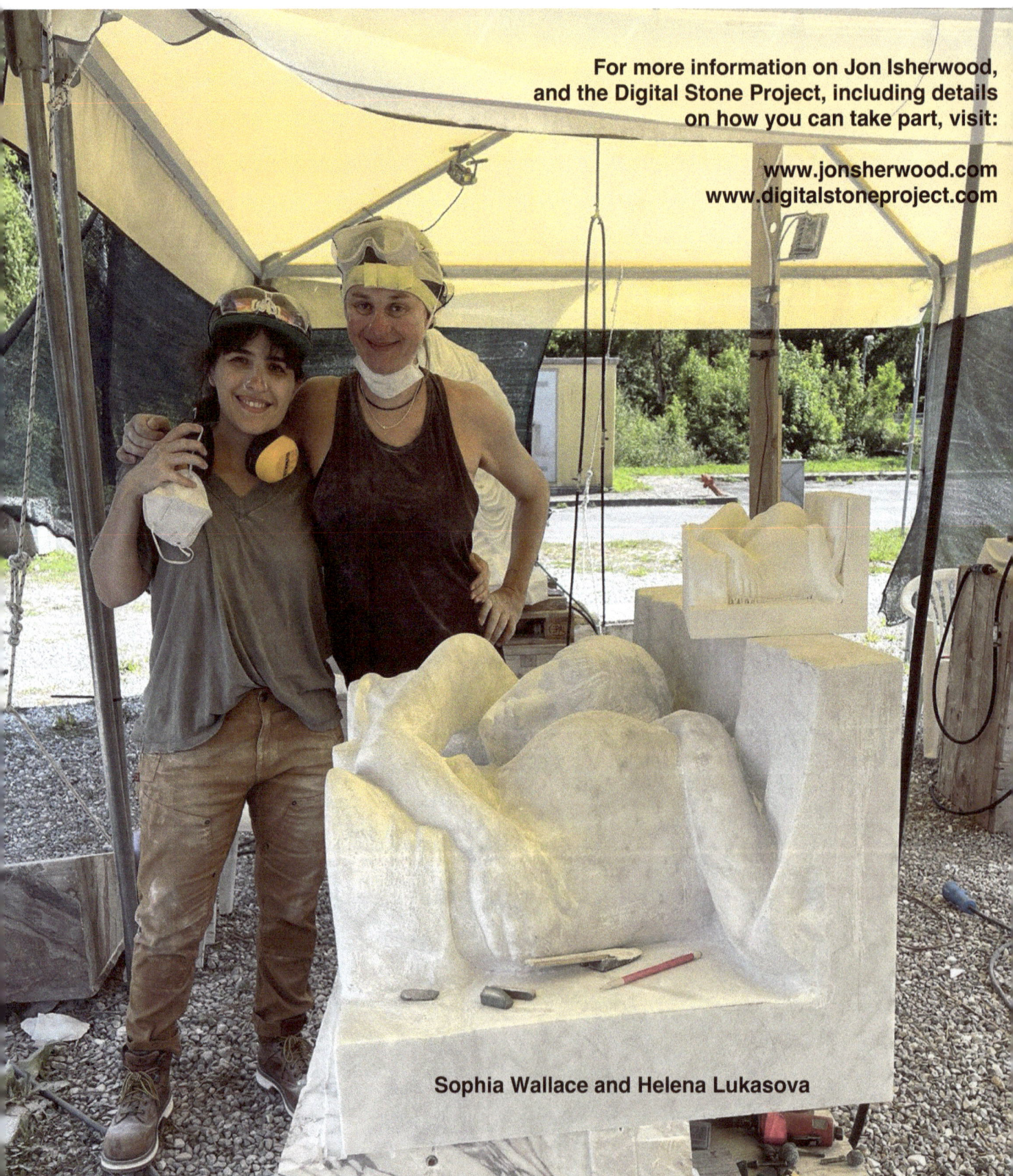

Sophia Wallace and Helena Lukasova

www.ingramcontent.com/pod-product-compliance
Lightning Source LLC
Chambersburg PA
CBHW041907240526
45473CB00040B/2969